LET EVERY HEART PREPARE HIM ROOM

LET EVERY HEART PREPARE HIM ROOM

Daily Family Devotions for Advent

NANCY GUTHRIE

Tyndale House Publishers, Inc.
CAROL STREAM, ILLINOIS

Visit Tyndale online at www.tyndale.com.

TYNDALE and Tyndale's quill logo are registered trademarks of Tyndale House Publishers, Inc.

Let Every Heart Prepare Him Room: Daily Family Devotions for Advent

The Library of Congress has catalogued the original edition as follows:

Guthrie, Nancy.
  Let every heart prepare Him room : daily family devotions for Advent / Nancy Guthrie.
     p. cm.
  ISBN 978-1-4143-3909-2 (hc)
  1. Advent—Prayers and devotions.   2. Families—Prayers and devotions.   I. Title.
  BV40.G88 2010
  242'.2—dc22   2010020828

Repackage first published in 2011 under ISBN 978-1-4143-6441-4

Printed in the United States of America

17 16 15 14 13 12 11
7   6   5   4   3   2   1

As December dawns, most families are busy putting Christmas programs and parties on the calendar, making holiday travel plans, and purchasing Christmas gifts. Those are all wonderful things, but if your family is anything like mine, these good things can squeeze out the best thing—nurturing a longing in our hearts and our homes for a fresh sense of wonder that God has come to us in Jesus. If we do not set aside time to focus together on what God's Word tells us about the promise of Christ, on Christmas morning we can find ourselves surrounded by mounds of torn gift wrap, our laps full of presents, but with hearts that are empty and unprepared.

As you enter into December this year, I hope you and your family will gather at some point each day to read this book and turn your focus to God's promise of a Savior. You'll be reminded of how God's people longed for centuries for the Messiah to come, and you'll read the Gospel accounts of the Messiah's coming. By setting aside this time, you'll turn away from this world's materialistic frenzy and toward a truly sacred celebration of Christ's coming.

Let Every Heart Prepare Him Room *provides a short reading for every day in the month of December, taking your family on a journey of identifying with the distant longings of Israel, listening for the angel's announcement, and gazing at the Baby in the manger. You'll find several suggested discussion questions that will help to transform this time into a meaningful discussion in which everybody in the family can participate. Each day's questions begin with a question that even the youngest member of the family can likely answer. There are additional Scriptures you might want to read as part of your discussion and Christmas songs your family can talk through and then sing together. Several lined pages have been spaced throughout the book where you can jot down dated notes of comments made and questions asked by various family members that you want to remember as the years go by.*

The busyness of December can easily crowd out contemplation of the amazing reality of God's coming to live among us as one of us. I hope that your family will overcome the empty busyness of this season and that in your home, every heart will prepare room for Jesus.

—*Nancy Guthrie*

When someone promises us something wonderful, we can hardly wait for that promise to be fulfilled. If the promise is something good, we want it *now*! We really don't like to wait. And yet the very best things are worth waiting for.

A long, long time ago, God made a promise to his people, Israel. In fact, he made many promises to them. But God's most important promise—the promise all his other promises depended on—was that he would send the Messiah, the Anointed One, who would save them from the difficulties of living life in this world broken by sin. The Messiah would not be an ordinary person, but God's own Son. The people he made the promise to had to wait, putting all their faith in the One who made the promise.

The season leading up to Christmas is called Advent, which means *coming*. During Advent, we remember the thousands of years God's chosen people anticipated and longed for the coming of God's salvation through the Messiah. Then, at Christmas, we celebrate the fulfillment of the promises God made. Jesus—the Savior God had promised—was born to us. No more waiting. Jesus came.

When John the Baptist was born, his father, Zechariah, recognized that the long years of waiting were finally over. God gave him a special understanding that his son, John, was going to prepare the way for the promised Messiah. Zechariah celebrated that God was about to fulfill his promise. He said, "Praise the Lord, the God of Israel, because he has visited and redeemed his people. He has sent us a mighty Savior from the royal line of his servant David, just as he promised through his holy prophets long ago" (Luke 1:68-70).

God promised that he would send a Savior, which he did when Jesus became a human baby. And while Jesus did everything necessary to save us when he came the first time, he also promised to come again. Then all God's promises will be completely fulfilled. So again we are waiting. Waiting patiently for God to fulfill his promises is what it means to have faith.

Putting faith in God's promises is not something a person does only one time on the day he or she becomes a Christian. The essence of being a Christian is placing all our hope in God, knowing we can trust him to fulfill all his promises—even the ones that haven't been fulfilled yet. We are willing to wait, trusting that "God's way is perfect. All the LORD's promises prove true" (Psalm 18:30).

PRAYER

Like your people of old, we are waiting for you,
God, to fulfill all your promises. And because we remember
how you fulfilled your promise to send Jesus,
we know that you will fulfill all your promises to us.

✦ ✦ ✦

Discussion Starters

- What does it mean to make a promise?

- Zechariah said that God would soon send a mighty Savior "as he promised through his holy prophets long ago." Look up these verses in your Bible to see a few examples of promises God made about the Messiah, given through his prophets in the Old Testament: Deuteronomy 18:15; Psalm 72:10; Isaiah 7:14; 9:6-7; Jeremiah 23:5-6.

- Waiting for Christmas to come gives us a tiny taste of what it must have been like for God's people to wait hundreds of years for God to fulfill his promise in sending Jesus. Why do you think it is good to learn to wait on God?

More from the Bible about—
THE PROMISED ONE:
Remember that Christ came as a servant to the Jews to show
that God is true to the promises he made to their ancestors.
ROMANS 15:8

All of God's promises have been fulfilled in Christ with a resounding
"Yes!" 2 CORINTHIANS 1:20

Right on Time

Most days we set specific times for when we will go to school, have piano lessons, or get picked up from our friend's house. But sometimes there is not a specific time set for something, and we're left waiting, wondering when the package will be delivered, when the plumber will arrive at our house, or when our ride is going to show up. We wonder if we've been forgotten.

By the time Jesus was born, the Jewish people had been waiting for hundreds of years for God to send his promised Messiah. It had been more than four hundred years since they had even heard God speak to them through one of his prophets about the Savior he would send. It seemed like God had stopped talking to them, and some people had grown weary of keeping up their hopes that God would come through for them. While they were waiting, the Romans occupied their country and ruled over them. This made them long even more for the great Deliverer God had promised.

Though it is hard to wait on God, and though it sometimes seems to us that God is slow, God's timing is always perfect. He is never late. He always acts at just the right time.

God knew when the time was just right to send Jesus, the Messiah, into the world. He knew when the exact religious, cultural, and political conditions were in place. Paul wrote, "*When the right time came*, God sent his Son, born of a woman" (Galatians 4:4, emphasis added). You see, God is not making up plans as he goes. All the grand events of God's plan for our redemption have been scheduled in advance, from Creation to the enslavement and exodus of God's people from Egypt; to David's taking the throne in Israel; to the birth, death, and resurrection of Jesus; to the day when Jesus will return. Paul said that God "has set a day for judging the world" (Acts 17:31). The course and timing of history is not a mystery to God. Time is in his hands, and he will bring about his plans and purposes in our world and in our lives right on time.

✦ ✦ ✦

Discussion Starters

- Describe a time when you had to wait for someone to show up. What was it like to wait?

- Can you think of some instances in the Bible when God said exactly how long something would last? For example, what did he say would last forty days (Genesis 7:4)? What did he say would last four hundred years (Genesis 15:13)? What did he say would last forty years (Numbers 14:34)? What does this show us about God's careful timing?

- How can understanding God's lordship over time help us to trust God's perfect timing for our lives?

More from the Bible about—
GOD'S TIMING IN SENDING JESUS:
Before John came, all the prophets and the law of Moses looked forward to this present time.   MATTHEW 11:13

"The time promised by God has come at last!" he announced. "The Kingdom of God is near! Repent of your sins and believe the Good News!"   MARK 1:15

O Come, O Come, Emmanuel

The writings of the prophet Isaiah inspired the hymn "O Come, O Come, Emmanuel." Long before the birth of Jesus, Isaiah prophesied about the Savior God would send, implanting in the hearts of God's people a longing for Immanuel (which is the Hebrew version of the Greek name Emmanuel). Hundreds of years before Jesus was born to the Virgin Mary, Isaiah wrote, "The virgin will conceive a child! She will give birth to a son and will call him Immanuel (which means 'God is with us')" (Isaiah 7:14).

Though it was hard for the people in Isaiah's day to imagine or understand how God would actually become a human, they began to long for this Messiah who would be "God with us." They looked forward to the day when God would fulfill all his promises by coming to live with them. We identify with them in their longing for God to fulfill his promise to send Jesus when we sing "O Come, O Come, Emmanuel."

To understand what this song is saying, we have to understand some of Israel's history. Remember that at one time God's people were slaves in Egypt and God brought them out, led by Moses. They wandered in the wilderness for forty years before finally entering into the land God had promised them. But God's people sinned and rebelled, and after a while, one part of the country was carried off into exile to Assyria and another to Babylon. Living far away from home, the people of God longed for him to come and rescue them from their captivity. As they sat in exile, many undoubtedly remembered the prophetic words of Isaiah. A child was coming who would save Israel—the Lord's presence in the flesh. We sing of their longing in the first verse:

O come, O come, Emmanuel, and ransom captive Israel,
that mourns in lonely exile here until the Son of God appear.
Rejoice! Rejoice! Emmanuel shall come to thee, O Israel!

When we sing the verse "O come, Thou Day-spring, come and cheer . . . ," it reminds us of Zechariah's prophecy: "The morning light from heaven is about to break upon us, to give light to those who sit in darkness and in the shadow of death" (Luke 1:78-79). In other words, Zechariah likened the coming Messiah to the rising sun, shining light upon the dark world (cf. John 1:1-5).

O come, Thou Day-spring, come and cheer our spirits by Thine
advent here;
Disperse the gloomy clouds of night, and death's dark shadows put
to flight.
Rejoice! Rejoice! Emmanuel shall come to thee, O Israel.

This song stirs in us a longing for Christ to come to fulfill his promises. The words prepare our hearts to truly celebrate Christmas when it comes. We are *preparing* for Christmas by purposefully nurturing in our hearts and in our homes a sacred longing for Christ to come.

Singing this song reminds us that the birth of Christ was not a surprising turn of events in history; it was the long-awaited fulfillment of God's promise to his people. As we sing it, we are encouraged that as he came before, he will come again! When he comes again, we'll hear a shout from the throne of God, saying, "Look, God's home is now among his people! He will live with them, and they will be his people. God himself will be with them" (Revelation 21:3). When he comes back, all the longings we sing about will be fulfilled. Finally and forever we will enjoy Emmanuel—God with us.

Remembering How God Has Prepared Our Hearts Year to Year

COMMENTS MADE AND QUESTIONS ASKED
DURING OUR FAMILY'S DEVOTIONS DURING ADVENT

_____

_____

_____

_____

_____

_____

_____

_____

_____

_____

_____

_____

_____

_____

_____

_____

_____

_____

_____

Family Matters

You might know people who can trace their ancestors to someone famous—a war hero, an inventor, a sports legend, or a Hollywood actor. People who are related to someone famous usually like to talk about it, but it is different when people can trace their ancestry to someone infamous for being a liar or murderer or thief. Descendants of these kinds of people are not usually so quick to want to talk about their ancestor.

But that is not the case with Jesus. The Gospels of Matthew and Luke both include a genealogy—a record of Jesus' human ancestry—and it includes some people known more for terrible sin than for something good. Matthew began his book this way: "This is a record of the ancestors of Jesus the Messiah, a descendant of David and of Abraham . . ." The list goes on for many generations and ends, "Jacob was the father of Joseph, the husband of Mary. Mary gave birth to Jesus, who is called the Messiah" (Matthew 1:1, 16). Luke traced Jesus' ancestry all the way back to Adam, beginning, "Jesus was known as the son of Joseph," and ending, "Adam was the son of God" (Luke 3:23, 38).

When we look through the list of people in Jesus' ancestral line, we see people famous for their faith—like Noah and Abraham and David. But we also see people with tarnished reputations—like Judah, who was intimate with his daughter-in-law; Rahab, who was a Canaanite prostitute; and Manasseh, the king who put false idols in the Temple. Even Noah, Abraham, and David, as faithful as they were, were sinners, and all of them needed a Savior.

We find hope in the ancestry of Jesus that no matter what we've done or where we come from, we too can be included in Jesus' family. Jesus does not look for people who are perfect and have never failed or made mistakes to be in his family. Instead, he is drawn toward people who recognize their failures and see their need for him.

PRAYER

*How grateful we are to know that you are not ashamed to have
sinners and failures in your own family, Jesus. When we look
at this record of your own family, we know that you are
not ashamed to have us in your family. Instead, you welcome us.*

✦ ✦ ✦

Discussion Starters

- What do you know about your ancestry—your grandparents and
  great-grandparents and great-great-grandparents? (Parents, do you
  have an interesting story you can share with your children about one
  of their ancestors?)

- Look through the two genealogies of Jesus, in Matthew 1 and Luke 3.
  What do you know about some of those people? Who are you
  surprised to see there because of what you know about them?

- Why does Luke 3:23 (NIV) say that Jesus was "the son, so it was
  thought, of Joseph," and why does that matter?

More from the Bible about—
BEING IN JESUS' FAMILY:
Anyone who does the will of my Father in heaven is my brother
and sister and mother!   MATTHEW 12:50

So now Jesus and the ones he makes holy have the same Father.
That is why Jesus is not ashamed to call them his brothers and
sisters.   HEBREWS 2:11

Getting and Giving

This is the season our mailboxes are filled with stacks of mail-order catalogs, and the television is full of advertisements of all kinds of shiny new things wrapped up with red bows. Through their colorful pictures and creative words, advertisers seek to convince us that we don't have enough stuff—that we need more, newer, better. It is their job to convince us to feel dissatisfied and discontented with what we have. They want to feed our natural desires for more than we really need.

So how will our family respond to all the messages around us this time of year? How can we make sure that Christmas in our house is about more than making lists of the stuff we want and figuring out what to give to other people? Do we really need to keep collecting more stuff and spending more money on ourselves? Can we stop believing the lie that the more we get, the more satisfied we'll be?

By putting our focus on giving to others and meeting their very real needs, we can battle the greed in our hearts. Christmas is a season not of getting, but of giving, because at Christmas we are celebrating that God is the most generous and outrageous Giver in the universe. After all, he gave us his Son. Proverbs says, "Some people are always greedy for more, but the godly love to give!" (Proverbs 21:26). To pour ourselves into becoming outrageous givers is to pursue becoming more like God. God turns greedy, grasping, fearful hoarders into generous, honest, cheerful givers.

To become givers, we have to decide not to listen to the voice inside us that tells us we must keep a tight grip on what we have so we will never be in need. We have to reject the lie that money in the bank and a pantry full of food takes care of our needs, remembering that ultimately it is God who takes care of all our needs. We have to tell ourselves the truth about God—that because he has been so generous in giving us Jesus, we can be confident that he will give us everything we need. We take him at his word, believing that he can satisfy us and that he will bless us as we give to others. We trust his promise that "it is more blessed to give than to receive" (Acts 20:35).

PRAYER

Generous, giving God, we want to put your word to the test this Christmas. We want to find out for ourselves how happy it will make us to give. We want to become generous givers like you are, confident that you will take care of all our needs.

✦ ✦ ✦

Discussion Starters

- What do you find yourself dreaming of getting? What do you find yourself dreaming of giving?

- When have you experienced or observed someone else enjoying the happiness that comes from outrageous giving?

- This Christmas, how can our family avoid the trap of making Christmas only about getting stuff?

More from the Bible about—
GIVING AND GREED:
Since [God] did not spare even his own Son but gave him up for us all, won't he also give us everything else? ROMANS 8:32

A greedy person is an idolater, worshiping the things of this world.
EPHESIANS 5:5

God Pitched His Tent

It can be great fun to put up a tent in your backyard to play in or sleep in. Imagine what it would be like for someone else to put up a tent in your backyard and begin living there—right in your backyard! In a sense, John says Jesus did just that. "So the Word became human and made his home among us" (John 1:14). The Greek word translated "made his home" is the word for "set up a tent." This verse is saying that God became a human person who set up his tent in our backyard and moved in.

If another family were to put up a tent in your backyard to live in, they would probably use your bathroom and have their meals around your table. They would be with you almost all the time, and no doubt their lives would intertwine with yours. This is what Jesus did when he became human. He made his home with us. He did this so that his life would be intertwined with ours—so that we would share our lives with him and so we could see him up close and really know him.

When we see God up close in the person of Jesus, what do we see? John wrote, "He was full of unfailing love and faithfulness" (John 1:14). Imagine having someone living with you who always loved perfectly and who was completely dependable to do what he said he would do. Doesn't that seem like the kind of person you would want to have making himself at home with your family?

John writes that many people of Jesus' day were not so happy to have Jesus right there with them. "He came to his own people, and even they rejected him. But to all who believed him and accepted him, he gave the right to become children of God" (John 1:11-12). While many rejected him, there were those who believed and accepted him. To believe and accept Jesus is to invite him to make his home with you and among you. It is to welcome him in, not as a guest, but as a permanent part of the family.

PRAYER
You have come, Jesus, to make your home among us.
And we welcome you! We believe you. We accept you.
Make yourself at home in our home.

✦ ✦ ✦

Discussion Starters

- When someone wants to sit by you at an event or spend the night at your house, what does that say about how that person feels about you?

- John describes God in the flesh as "full of unfailing love and faithfulness." Do you think that is how most people see Jesus?

- What difference would it make if our family lived as if Jesus had made himself "at home" in our house?

More from the Bible about—
GOD MAKING HIS HOME WITH US:
I heard a loud shout from the throne, saying, "Look, God's home is now among his people! He will live with them, and they will be his people. God himself will be with them." REVELATION 21:3

Remembering How God Has Prepared Our Hearts Year to Year

COMMENTS MADE AND QUESTIONS ASKED
DURING OUR FAMILY'S DEVOTIONS DURING ADVENT

_____

_____

_____

_____

_____

_____

_____

_____

_____

_____

_____

_____

_____

_____

_____

_____

_____

_____

_____

I Am the Lord's Servant

It's hard to imagine how frightening it must have been for teenage Mary to see an angel and hear him speaking to her. The Bible says that "Gabriel appeared to her and said, 'Greetings, favored woman! The Lord is with you!' Confused and disturbed, Mary tried to think what the angel could mean. 'Don't be afraid, Mary,' the angel told her, 'for you have found favor with God!'" (Luke 1:28-30). We can't help but wonder what the angel looked like and what he sounded like.

As frightening as it must have been to see and hear an angel speaking to her, it must have been even more frightening for Mary to process what the angel was telling her—that she was going to become pregnant, even though she had never been intimate with a man. This would be a scandal in her village. Everyone would whisper about her. She would be shunned and perhaps sent away by her fiancé, Joseph, because he would think she had been unfaithful to him. And yet, even though she probably had a million questions and concerns, Mary responded to the angel by welcoming whatever God wanted to do. She said, "I am the Lord's servant. May everything you have said about me come true" (Luke 1:38). In a sense she said to God, "I'm yours. You can do anything you want with me," even though she must have known that this situation would be very hard for her, for Joseph, and for her whole family.

It's easy to label what we consider "good things" in our lives as gifts from God and to welcome them with gratitude. But when difficult things happen, we don't look at them as part of God's good plan for us. Mary's example shows us we can also welcome those things we would not necessarily label "good," confident that God's gifts sometimes come in perplexing and even painful packages. When we belong to God, we know he will use whatever he allows into our lives for good. Somehow, in God's hands, these things also become gifts of his grace toward us.

It takes faith—faith to rest in who God is and his love for us; faith to be confident that he is doing something good in and through our difficult circumstances—to see the hard things in our lives as gifts of God's grace.

PRAYER

God, give us faith to surrender ourselves to you even in the hard places of life. We want to be your servants. We believe that anything you ask of us will be good and right because you love us. Fill us with faith to trust you with whatever you ask of us.

✦ ✦ ✦

Discussion Starters

- What thoughts do you think went through Mary's mind when the angel was speaking to her?

- What did Mary believe about God and his promises that allowed her to respond with a song of praise?

- What difficult things has God asked our family to do or endure? How might these difficult things be God's gifts to us?

More from the Bible about—
MARY'S RESPONSE TO THIS NEWS:
How my spirit rejoices in God my Savior! For he took notice of his lowly servant girl, and from now on all generations will call me blessed. For the Mighty One is holy, and he has done great things for me. . . . He has helped his servant Israel and remembered to be merciful. For he made this promise to our ancestors, to Abraham and his children forever. LUKE 1:47-49, 54-55

Name Him Jesus

Most parents spend a lot of time thinking about what they will name their babies. They think through names with special meanings, traditional family names, and names they just like.

It was common in the time when Jesus was born for parents to give their baby the name of someone in the family. But this is not what Mary and Joseph did. They didn't have to make a list of possibilities of what they might name the baby. An angel appeared separately to Mary and then to Joseph, telling each of them exactly what name to give the baby.

To Mary the angel said, "You will conceive and give birth to a son, and you will name him Jesus" (Luke 1:31). The angel also spoke to Joseph in a dream, saying, "Joseph, son of David . . . do not be afraid to take Mary as your wife. For the child within her was conceived by the Holy Spirit. And she will have a son, and you are to name him Jesus, for he will save his people from their sins" (Matthew 1:20-21).

The name *Jesus* was no random name, though it was an ordinary name for a Jewish boy in that day. The name *Jesus* was rich with meaning about who this child would be and what he would do.

Jesus (*Yeshua* in Hebrew) means "the LORD saves." It is a combination of *Yahu*, a personal name for God, and *shua*, which means "a cry for help" or "a saving cry." So by this name the angel was telling Joseph and Mary that this child would be a rescuer, a savior—someone who would prove to be no less than God himself in the body of a baby.

Jesus' very name tells us why he came and why his coming was such cause for celebration that we still celebrate his coming today. Jesus is "the LORD saves." He has come to rescue us from the sin that would keep us apart from God for eternity.

PRAYER

Yeshua, thank you for being the God who saves. We know we cannot save ourselves and that there is no one and nothing else that can save us. We turn to you and believe that you are strong enough and good enough to save us.

✦ ✦ ✦

Discussion Starters

– What does your name mean? (Parents, you may want to take a moment to explain to your children why you chose the name you did.)

– Jesus' name is "the LORD saves," and later the angel says to the shepherds that a "Savior" has been born. What does it mean that Jesus is the Savior? What does he save us from?

– What do you think it was like for Mary and Joseph to think about their baby as the "the LORD saves"?

More from the Bible about—
THE NAME OF JESUS:
At the name of Jesus every knee should bow, in heaven and on earth and under the earth, and every tongue confess that Jesus Christ is Lord, to the glory of God the Father.   PHILIPPIANS 2:10-11

Jesus is the one referred to in the Scriptures, where it says, "The stone that you builders rejected has now become the cornerstone." There is salvation in no one else! God has given no other name under heaven by which we must be saved.   ACTS 4:11-12

People like to try to guess about babies even before they are born—boy or girl, shy or rambunctious, athletic or artful. But, of course, we don't know what a baby will be like until he or she is here.

While there were certainly many things Mary and Joseph did not know about the baby Mary was carrying, the angel Gabriel told them some amazing things about him. "He will be very great and will be called the Son of the Most High. The Lord God will give him the throne of his ancestor David. And he will reign over Israel forever; his Kingdom will never end!" (Luke 1:32-33). It must have been more than Mary could take in or understand.

The angel said that Jesus would be "very great." Who do you think is great? Whoever it is, Jesus is greater. All the smartest people of our day would have to sit at the feet of Jesus to learn from him. All the bravest military men of our day would want to follow behind him. All the greatest musicians would be hushed at the beauty of his music. Jesus is very great.

The angel Gabriel also said that Jesus "will be called the Son of the Most High." This is different from when God refers to the nation of Israel as his "firstborn son" (Exodus 4:22) and Christians as "sons of the Most High" (Luke 6:35, NIV). The angel was saying that Jesus would be *the* Son of the Most High God. This child would not be an ordinary person, but the one and only Son of God become human. Mary was carrying the Son of God inside her body!

Then Gabriel said, "The Lord God will give him the throne of his ancestor David." It might be hard for *us* to understand why this was a big deal, but Mary knew why. Her son was going to be a king—but not just any king. Jesus, a descendant of King David, would be the descendant whom God had promised hundreds of years before who would finally make things right for God's people. God had promised King David, "I will raise up one of your descendants, your own offspring, and I will make his kingdom strong. . . . I will secure his royal throne forever. . . . Your kingdom will continue before me for all time, and your throne will be secure forever" (2 Samuel 7:12-13, 16). Mary's baby would finally fulfill this promise!

Obviously this King would be different from all other kings, who come and go. Gabriel said, "He will reign over Israel forever; his Kingdom will never end!" *Never end?* Even now, King Jesus is on the throne of the universe. Though we can't see this with our eyes, we know it is true. But one day we *will* see it with our eyes, and every person will bow before King Jesus!

PRAYER

King Jesus, we bow before you now, believing that you are
very great and worthy of our worship. We long for the day when
your Kingdom comes and your will is done on earth as it is in
heaven. May you be the King of our home this day,
and King of our hearts forever.

✦ ✦ ✦

Discussion Starters

- *Who is someone you think of as great? What makes him or her great?*

- *Read Luke 1:31-33. Can you memorize five things the angel told Mary about her child?*

- *What do you think it was like for Mary to take in what the angel told her about what her baby would do and who he would be?*

More from the Bible about—
THE NAME OF JESUS:
He will be called: Wonderful Counselor, Mighty God, Everlasting Father, Prince of Peace. His government and its peace will never end. He will rule with fairness and justice from the throne of his ancestor David for all eternity.   ISAIAH 9:6-7

Jesus was standing before Pilate, the Roman governor. "Are you the king of the Jews?" the governor asked him. Jesus replied, "You have said it."   MATTHEW 27:11

I am both the source of David and the heir to his throne.
REVELATION 22:16

Remembering How God Has Prepared Our Hearts Year to Year

COMMENTS MADE AND QUESTIONS ASKED
DURING OUR FAMILY'S DEVOTIONS DURING ADVENT

_____

_____

_____

_____

_____

_____

_____

_____

_____

_____

_____

_____

_____

_____

_____

_____

_____

_____

Overshadowed

If you have ever driven through thick fog—so thick you could barely see what was in front of you—you know it can be kind of scary. Fog is basically a cloud close to the ground. In several places in the Bible, the presence and power of God in the person of the Holy Spirit is described as a cloud in which God came close to earth—but it usually didn't scare people. In the second verse of the Bible we read that "the earth was formless and empty, and darkness covered the deep waters. And the Spirit of God was hovering over the surface of the waters" (Genesis 1:2). The Holy Spirit hovered over the unformed earth like a cloud. Later, God's presence, like a cloud, led the Israelites in the desert (Exodus 13:21). We also read about a bright, shining cloud that came down when Jesus was on the top of a mountain with three of his disciples and that "a voice from the cloud said, 'This is my dearly loved Son, who brings me great joy. Listen to him'" (Matthew 17:5).

We get that same sense of an enveloping cloud of the presence of God when we read the words the angel said to Mary: "The Holy Spirit will come upon you, and the power of the Most High will overshadow you. So the baby to be born will be holy, and he will be called the Son of God" (Luke 1:35).

The angel said that the Holy Spirit would "come upon" Mary and "overshadow" her, similar to the way a cloud might. God, in the person of the Holy Spirit, would come over her and do a creative work in her womb, making new life.

While Mary's experience was certainly unique, we all desperately need the Holy Spirit to come upon us and overshadow us. We need him to make new life where there is deadness in our spirits, to bring light where there is darkness in our hearts. We need the Holy Spirit to enter into the chaos of our inner thoughts, emotions, and desires and change us from the inside out. We can't create new spiritual life on our own. We need the power of God to work inside us so that Christ can be born in us.

PRAYER

Holy Spirit, come and overshadow our home like a cloud.
Make us aware of your constant presence
that guides us and gives us life.

✦ ✦ ✦

Discussion Starters

– What is it like to be in the middle of a cloud in the form of fog?

– What do you know about the work of the Holy Spirit? What difference does he make when he lives inside a person?

– If the Holy Spirit were to permeate our home, what effect might he have?

More from the Bible about—
THE OVERSHADOWING OF THE HOLY SPIRIT:
You will receive power when the Holy Spirit comes upon you. And you will be my witnesses, telling people about me everywhere— in Jerusalem, throughout Judea, in Samaria, and to the ends of the earth.   ACTS 1:8

The Spirit alone gives eternal life. Human effort accomplishes nothing. And the very words I have spoken to you are spirit and life.   JOHN 6:63

The Spirit of God, who raised Jesus from the dead, lives in you. And just as God raised Christ Jesus from the dead, he will give life to your mortal bodies by this same Spirit living within you.
ROMANS 8:11

Jump for Joy

One of the most exciting times in a woman's pregnancy is when she begins to feel her child move inside her. It all becomes more real as the mother begins to feel the baby shift positions, move an arm or leg, or even hiccup.

When the angel told Zechariah that his wife, Elizabeth, would have a son named John who would prepare people to receive the Messiah, he said that this baby would be "filled with the Holy Spirit, even before his birth" (Luke 1:15). And when Elizabeth was six months pregnant, her relative Mary came to visit. When Mary, carrying Jesus in her womb, walked in, something amazing happened. Luke wrote:

> At the sound of Mary's greeting, Elizabeth's child leaped within her, and Elizabeth was filled with the Holy Spirit. Elizabeth gave a glad cry and exclaimed to Mary, "God has blessed you above all women, and your child is blessed. Why am I so honored, that the mother of my Lord should visit me? When I heard your greeting, the baby in my womb jumped for joy." (Luke 1:41-44)

It must have taken Elizabeth's breath away when she sensed the growing baby in her belly have a physical response to Mary's walking toward her. Elizabeth could feel her baby's excitement, and she knew why he was excited. Luke said, "Elizabeth was filled with the Holy Spirit." Both mother and child were filled with the Holy Spirit, and the Spirit enabled them to sense the presence of the Messiah in Mary's womb.

The Holy Spirit helps us recognize that we need Jesus to save us. In fact, he's the only way we can respond to Jesus. We could never do it on our own. And when the Holy Spirit softens our hearts to welcome Jesus in, we, like the baby in Elizabeth's womb, jump for joy!

PRAYER

Lord, fill us with your Spirit so that throughout this Christmas
season we will jump for joy at your coming.

✦ ✦ ✦

Discussion Starters

- Describe a time when you have been so happy and excited that you
  jumped for joy (or wished you could have).

- What do you think the conversations between Elizabeth and Mary
  would have been like when Mary came to visit?

- What other examples can you think of from the Bible when the Spirit
  gave someone the ability to recognize who Jesus was?

More from the Bible about—
JOY IN THE PRESENCE OF JESUS:
What blessings await you when people hate you and exclude you
and mock you and curse you as evil because you follow the Son
of Man. When that happens, be happy! Yes, leap for joy! For a
great reward awaits you in heaven. And remember, their ancestors
treated the ancient prophets that same way.   LUKE 6:22-23

There is more joy in heaven over one lost sinner who repents and
returns to God than over ninety-nine others who are righteous and
haven't strayed away!   LUKE 15:7

The Holy Spirit produces this kind of fruit in our lives: love, joy . . .
GALATIANS 5:22

Magnification

As Mary thought through what the angel told her and considered how amazing it was that God had chosen her—an ordinary person—to be the human mother of God's Son, she broke out into a song: "Oh, how my soul praises the Lord. How my spirit rejoices in God my Savior! For he took notice of his lowly servant girl, and from now on all generations will call me blessed" (Luke 1:46-48).

Another Bible translation says that Mary said, "My soul *magnifies* the Lord" (NKJV, emphasis added). What did she mean by *magnifies*?

When you look at something through a magnifying glass, it looks much bigger than it actually is. Is that what Mary meant when she said, "My soul magnifies the Lord"? Was she trying to make God look bigger than he actually is?

We can never make God bigger or greater than he is. The truth is, we can never fully take in or understand God's greatness. But we can magnify him. We magnify God not by making him bigger than he truly is, but by making him greater in our thoughts, in our affections, in our memories, and in our expectations. We magnify him by having higher, larger, and truer thoughts of him. We magnify him by praising him and telling others about his greatness so they can have bigger thoughts about him too.

Sometimes we wonder why we aren't happy, why we make sinful choices, why we feel distant from God. Often it's because we have small thoughts about God and magnified thoughts of ourselves, our wants, our rights, our accomplishments. Mary, the one God chose to be the mother of his Son, could have easily allowed her thoughts of herself to become larger, even prideful. But instead of magnifying herself, she magnified the Lord.

Lord, deep in our souls, we choose to magnify you today.
We want to magnify you in our home—in our conversations and
in our hearts. Forgive us for our small thoughts of you.
May you be magnified!

✦ ✦ ✦

Discussion Starters

- What is the most interesting thing you've looked at through a magnifying glass?

- Read Luke 1:46-55. What are some phrases that show Mary's humble thoughts about herself and her big thoughts about God?

- What are some ways our family can magnify God in how we anticipate and celebrate Christmas?

More from the Bible about—
THOSE WHO SOUGHT TO MAGNIFY JESUS:
Oh, magnify the LORD with me, and let us exalt His name together.
PSALM 34:3, NKJV

I will praise the name of God with a song, and will magnify Him with thanksgiving. PSALM 69:30, NKJV

Remembering How God Has Prepared Our Hearts Year to Year

COMMENTS MADE AND QUESTIONS ASKED
DURING OUR FAMILY'S DEVOTIONS DURING ADVENT

_____

_____

_____

_____

_____

_____

_____

_____

_____

_____

_____

_____

_____

_____

_____

_____

_____

_____

_____

Bethlehem was a small and unimpressive village, but the prophet Micah had given an amazing prophecy about this little town. "You, O Bethlehem Ephrathah, are only a small village among all the people of Judah. Yet a ruler of Israel will come from you, one whose origins are from the distant past. . . . And he will stand to lead his flock with the LORD's strength" (Micah 5:2, 4).

It had been over four hundred years since Micah wrote this prophecy. The Jewish people knew this prophecy, and they knew that the Messiah would be a descendant of King David, who was from Bethlehem (1 Samuel 16:1). But even so, many people of Jesus' day were surprised that their Savior would be born as a baby in such a small, unremarkable village.

For some reason, people tend to be surprised when someone from a small town accomplishes something of true greatness. We have a tendency to think that for something or someone to be significant, the idea, the business, or the person must be born and raised in a major city or a well-known place and must be from a well-known or well-off family.

When God sent Jesus, he turned upside down every expectation of what people thought would make him great. Jesus came as a baby instead of a grown man. He was born to ordinary parents, not people of prominence or power. He came as a humble teacher rather than a conquering king. And he was born in an obscure little town rather than one of the great cities of the day.

This tells us something important about how God chooses the people he will use and bless. He doesn't choose on the basis of accomplishments or reputation or worldly value. God chooses to use simple, ordinary things and people so that he is the one who gets all the glory.

PRAYER

*Child of Bethlehem, we are grateful to know that
you came to ordinary people in an ordinary place,
because we are ordinary. May your glory shine bright
in this ordinary place we call home.*

✦ ✦ ✦

Discussion Starters

- Think of someone famous you know or have read about who came from a small town.

- What are some of the ways we show that we believe bigger is better?

- Bethlehem means "house of bread," and it was King David's hometown. Why are these two facts significant for the place of Jesus' birth?

More from the Bible about—
HOW GOD USES ORDINARY THINGS FOR HIS SIGNIFICANT PURPOSE:
God, who said, "Let there be light in the darkness," has made this light shine in our hearts so we could know the glory of God that is seen in the face of Jesus Christ. We now have this light shining in our hearts, but we ourselves are like fragile clay jars containing this great treasure. This makes it clear that our great power is from God, not from ourselves. 2 CORINTHIANS 4:6-7

O Little Town of Bethlehem

1. O little town of Bethlehem, how still we see thee lie! Above thy deep and dreamless sleep the silent stars go by. Yet in thy dark streets shineth the everlasting Light; The hopes and fears of all the years are met in thee tonight.

2. For Christ is born of Mary, and gathered all above, While mortals sleep, the angels keep their watch of wond'ring love. O morning stars together, proclaim the holy birth, And praises sing to God the King, and peace to men on earth!

3. How silently, how silently, the wondrous Gift is giv'n; So God imparts to human hearts the blessings of His Heav'n. No ear may hear His coming, but in this world of sin, Where meek souls will receive Him still, the dear Christ enters in.

The writer of this song, Phillips Brooks, depicted Bethlehem as "still" and resting silently in "deep and dreamless sleep." And yet we know that on the night Christ was born, Bethlehem was not still or silent. It was crowded with people because of the census. There was no place for Joseph and Mary to stay, and probably the streets were full of people.

Most likely Brooks was thinking of Bethlehem not as it was on the night Jesus was born, but at the time the prophet Micah wrote about this little village: "You, O Bethlehem Ephrathah, are only a small village among all the people of Judah. Yet a ruler of Israel will come from you, one whose origins are from the distant past" (Micah 5:2). Micah prophesied that a day would come when this insignificant little town would see the birth of a mighty ruler, the promised Messiah.

When the writer of this carol penned, "Yet in thy dark streets shineth the everlasting Light," he depicted a scene of a dark night in Bethlehem and people who were utterly oblivious to the significance of what was taking place. The Son of God was born, and a light dawned that most of the people living there did not see and could not comprehend. But there, on that night, the one who would later say "I am the light of the world" broke through the darkness of this world.

While the writer of this carol takes us to the dark streets of this sleepy town, he also helps us to see what is happening in the heavens around Bethlehem—what human eyes cannot see. "While mortals sleep, the angels keep their watch of wond'ring love. O morning stars together, proclaim the holy birth. . . .We hear the Christmas angels the great glad tidings tell." This helps us see what is unseen—all of heaven bending down to see what God was doing as he brought Jesus into this world. The angels looked on in awe and wonder, helping us to see the wonder of it all.

So this carol focuses our eyes on the earthly town of Bethlehem, then the heavenly realm of angels, and finally, on our own hearts: "God imparts to human hearts the blessings of His Heav'n." This promise is offered to "meek souls" who "will receive Him still." And that is what we want to have this Advent season—souls that are marked by meekness, making us receptive to Christ.

It is one thing for us to read about the coming of Jesus and consider it as historical reality or even spiritual truth. But it is something else to truly engage with this reality and truth, to consciously invite this Child of Bethlehem to be "born in us"—to dwell in us by his Spirit. So as we sing this song, we're not just singing about a little town in which Jesus was born. We're singing a song of invitation to Jesus himself, throwing open the doors of our hearts, welcoming him to be born in our lives. The final verse, not included in the setting on page 34, gives us words to invite the wonder of this reality to penetrate our own lives and become real and meaningful to us. As you sing this song as a family, be sure to add the final verse, offering it as a prayer from your hearts:

> *O holy Child of Bethlehem, descend to us, we pray.*
> *Cast out our sin and enter in; be born in us today.*
> *We hear the Christmas angels the great glad tidings tell.*
> *O come to us, abide with us, our Lord Emmanuel!*

prepare the Way

What happens at your house when guests are coming? Do you clean up things that are messy, fix things that are broken, make plans for how you will welcome your visitors? As God prepared to send his Son into the world, he sent someone to get things ready. He had promised to do that, so some people were watching for this special individual.

Two Old Testament prophets (Malachi and Isaiah) had prophesied that before the Messiah would come, God would send a messenger to prepare the people. Malachi wrote, "Look! I am sending my messenger, and he will prepare the way before me. . . . Look, I am sending you the prophet Elijah" (Malachi 3:1; 4:5). Isaiah had written, "Listen! It's the voice of someone shouting, 'Clear the way through the wilderness for the LORD! Make a straight highway through the wasteland for our God!'" (Isaiah 40:3). Mark recorded, "This messenger was John the Baptist" (Mark 1:4). Luke wrote, "He will be a man with the spirit and power of Elijah. He will prepare the people for the coming of the Lord. He will turn the hearts of the fathers to their children, and he will cause those who are rebellious to accept the wisdom of the godly" (Luke 1:17).

John the Baptist was the person God sent to prepare his people for Jesus. It wasn't food or beds that needed to be prepared; it was hearts. It was John's mission to call people to repent—to leave behind their sin and turn back to God. John prepared the people for Jesus by helping them get their hearts ready to receive him.

God knows our hearts need to be prepared to receive Jesus. During December we tend to get very busy preparing for Christmas with parties and programs and presents. But the most important preparation we need to make is to prepare our hearts to welcome Jesus in a fresh, new way. We do this by cleaning out the clutter of sinful attitudes and selfishness so that we look expectantly for Jesus to make himself known to us.

PRAYER

Right now, Lord Jesus, our hearts are being prepared to receive you. Show us what must be removed, the sin that must be repented of, so that our hearts can fully receive you.

✦ ✦ ✦

Discussion Starters

– When Luke said that John came with the "spirit and power of Elijah," he meant that John proclaimed judgment for sin and called for repentance. How does an awareness of our sin help prepare us for Jesus?

– What happens when we refuse or neglect to prepare the way for Jesus to come to us?

– As we think about what we do to prepare for company, what similar things can we do to prepare to welcome Jesus into our home this Christmas?

More from the Bible about—
WELCOMING JESUS:
He came into the very world he created, but the world didn't recognize him. He came to his own people, and even they rejected him. But to all who believed him and accepted him, he gave the right to become children of God. JOHN 1:10-12

No Room for Him

Israel was an occupied country, and the people were forced to pay high taxes to the Roman emperor Caesar Augustus. To make sure he was getting as much in taxes as possible, Caesar took a census to count all the people living in every part of the empire, including Israel. All the people had to go to their ancestral hometowns to be counted. When all the people who were descendants of David arrived in the tiny town of Bethlehem to be counted, people made room in their houses for close relatives, and the places for travelers to stay filled up quickly. So when Mary and Joseph arrived in Bethlehem, the town was full so they had to nestle themselves into a place ordinarily used to house animals. While Mary and Joseph were in Bethlehem, "the time came for her baby to be born. She gave birth to her first child, a son. She . . . laid him in a manger, because there was no lodging available for them" (Luke 2:6-7).

We might think that since God could orchestrate an empire-wide census to bring Mary and Joseph to Bethlehem, surely he could have made sure there was a room available for Jesus to be born in. But somehow it seems appropriate that Jesus' life on earth would begin this way. Later Jesus said, "Foxes have dens to live in, and birds have nests, but the Son of Man has no place even to lay his head" (Matthew 8:20). Jesus never had a home of his own. His own people rejected him, and finally they crucified him because they refused to make room in their hearts to love and obey him.

Jesus never forces himself on us or into any area of our lives where we do not welcome him. So if we want Jesus to move in, we have to make room for him. We have to clear other things—even good things—out of our schedules if we want to make time to listen to him by reading his Word and talking to him through prayer. We have to make room in our thoughts for him, finding quiet times to focus on him, not just in this busy Christmas season, but all year long. When we open the door to Jesus and welcome him in, he makes himself at home in our hearts.

PRAYER

*Jesus, we want to make room for you in our home and in our hearts,
and we know that doing so may mean changing our schedules or
changing our habits. Show us what needs to be moved out so there
will be plenty of room for you to dwell here with us.*

✦ ✦ ✦

Discussion Starters

- What do you think it would be like to spend the night sleeping where
  animals are kept?

- Why do you think Jesus lived a life of poverty rather than one of
  comfort and financial means?

- What would it mean to make more room for Jesus in our schedules,
  our hearts, our home?

More from the Bible about—
MAKING ROOM FOR JESUS:
I correct and discipline everyone I love. So be diligent and turn from
your indifference. Look! I stand at the door and knock. If you hear
my voice and open the door, I will come in, and we will share a meal
together as friends.   REVELATION 3:19-20

Away in a Manger

1. A way in a man - ger, no
2. The cat - tle are low - ing, the
3. Be near me, Lord Je - sus, I

crib for a bed, The lit - tle Lord
Ba - by a - wakes, But lit - tle Lord
ask Thee to stay Close by me for -

Je - sus laid down His sweet head. The
Je - sus, no cry - ing He makes; I
ev - er, and love me, I pray; Bless

stars in the sky looked
love Thee, Lord Je - sus, look
all the dear chil - dren in

down where He lay, The lit - tle Lord
down from the sky And stay by my
Thy ten - der care, And fit us for

Je - sus, a - sleep on the hay.
cra - dle till morn - ing is nigh.
heav - en to live with Thee there.

We often think of this song as a Christmas carol sung by children, not only because of its depiction of the baby Jesus, but also because it talks about little children going to sleep in their cradles at night with the Savior Jesus watching over them. But actually this song was written more for a mother to sing over her children. It is her prayer for them, based on Luke's account that Mary "gave birth to her first child, a son. She wrapped him snugly in strips of cloth and laid him in a manger" (Luke 2:7).

The simplicity of this verse portrays the most staggering truth of all time—that God became a baby. The God of the universe, the Lord of glory, the one who created the heavens and the earth, the one who sustains all things by the power of his word, poured himself into the flesh of an infant. He wasn't born into a royal household of comfort and cleanliness, but came in the lowliest of ways to the lowliest of people. The very God who spoke "Let there be light" and there was light set aside the privileges and power of deity to become a baby who needed his mother. We've sung this carol so many times that we may barely even consider what this means. But this concept is unimaginable, incomprehensible: God became a baby.

We don't know who wrote this carol, and we don't know what the author meant by, "But little Lord Jesus, no crying He makes." Certainly Jesus cried as a baby. He was completely human, and human babies cry. We can never think that because Jesus was fully God, he somehow did not feel what humans feel. In fact, we know that Jesus cried as an adult. He wept over Jerusalem because they would not accept him. And he wept at the tomb of his friend Lazarus. So when we sing "no crying He makes," we should assume that this song's writer was giving us a snapshot of a peaceful scene in Bethlehem, as if the writer looked upon the young couple with their baby in the manger. The baby, at least at that moment, was content and not crying.

But the scene changes dramatically at the end of the second stanza, when we sing, "I love Thee, Lord Jesus, look down from the sky." We've been focusing on the baby Jesus sleeping in the cradle, but now the Lord Jesus is looking down from the sky.

That's because the mother singing this prayer over her sleeping children has moved her gaze from the picture of Jesus born as a baby in Bethlehem to where Jesus is now—risen from the dead, ascended to the right hand of God. Her prayer is not to a helpless baby, but to the risen, ascended King Jesus, and she is asking him to protect her sleeping child, to "stay by my cradle till morning is nigh."

The third stanza was added to this song sometime after the other stanzas were first written, and it moves from praying for the protecting presence of Christ to praying for the transforming work of Christ. The praying mother asks Jesus to "fit us for heaven to live with Thee there." She knows that on our own we are not fit for heaven. Without the transforming work of Christ in our lives, we simply cannot expect to live with Christ in the holiness of heaven. So this mother's prayer is that Christ would not only watch over her children while they sleep, but that he would also draw them to himself, making them "fit" for heaven.

Perhaps your family will want to sing the first two verses of "Away in a Manger" together, and then let Mom and Dad sing the final verse over the children. Children, hear this as the cry of your parents' hearts. Nothing is more important to your mom and dad than that Christ would work in your hearts and lives, doing what only Christ can do—make you fit for heaven by giving you his own righteousness, which you can receive only by faith.

Remembering How God Has Prepared Our Hearts Year to Year

COMMENTS MADE AND QUESTIONS ASKED
DURING OUR FAMILY'S DEVOTIONS DURING ADVENT

_____

_____

_____

_____

_____

_____

_____

_____

_____

_____

_____

_____

_____

_____

_____

_____

_____

_____

Clothed in Humility

Most of us like to look good. We realize that what we wear sends a message about us, and we want other people to think well of us. So we look for clothes that will tell people what we want to say about who we are, where we've come from, and what is important to us.

Long before Jesus was born—before he even created the world—he existed with God in all his heavenly glory. But Jesus chose to leave heaven and his robes of glory. He laid them aside to be wrapped in rags.

Mary didn't have nice clothes to put on Jesus when he was born in Bethlehem. In fact, there were no clothes at all for him—just strips of cloth that were wrapped around him. Luke wrote, "She gave birth to her first child, a son. She wrapped him snugly in strips of cloth and laid him in a manger" (Luke 2:7). So from the day he was born, Jesus' clothing told us something significant about who he is and what he is like. The way he was dressed reflected the type of man he would grow up to be—humble and lowly.

We see something similar in another scene much later in Jesus' life. The night before he died, Jesus took off his robe and wrapped a towel around his waist. Then he began to wash the dusty feet of his disciples. This was "servant work," an act of deep humility and service. When Jesus finished, he told them, "I have given you an example to follow" (John 13:15). This is the way all those who are disciples of Jesus are called to dress—in the clothing of a humble servant.

Throughout his life and as he faced death, Jesus showed us what it looks like to clothe ourselves in humility—not only in terms of actual clothing but in the inner attitudes of our hearts. "He took the humble position of a slave" (Philippians 2:7) instead of seeking to impress. When we choose to clothe ourselves in this way, we reveal that we are not out to impress, but to serve.

PRAYER

We want to be clothed in humility, Jesus, just like you. We want
to please you, God, more than we seek to impress other people.
Thank you, Jesus, for taking the humble position of a slave so
that you might serve us and show us how to serve others.

✦ ✦ ✦

Discussion Starters

- Think about your favorite outfit. Why do you like it, and what does it say about you?

- Think through Jesus' life and lifestyle. In addition to the way he dressed, what are some other signs that showed his humility?

- What does Philippians 2:3-8 teach us about Jesus' humility? How can we "clothe" ourselves the same way he does?

More from the Bible about—
WHAT IT MEANS TO BE CLOTHED IN HUMILITY:
Since God chose you to be the holy people he loves, you must
clothe yourselves with tenderhearted mercy, kindness, humility,
gentleness, and patience. **COLOSSIANS 3:12**

Don't be concerned about the outward beauty of fancy hair-
styles, expensive jewelry, or beautiful clothes. You should clothe
yourselves instead with the beauty that comes from within, the
unfading beauty of a gentle and quiet spirit, which is so precious
to God. **1 PETER 3:3-4**

Good News of Great Joy

Some people think anything having to do with God is very serious and could never be outrageously happy. They assume that doing things for God, studying about God, going to church and worshiping God, or even just thinking about God will be really boring and no fun. But Jesus is not a bore or a burden; he's not a drag or drudgery. Jesus is the greatest joy in the universe! He's the best news anyone has ever heard! In fact, nothing in all the world can give people as much joy as Jesus can.

That's what the angel told the shepherds who were taking care of their sheep on that dark night outside Bethlehem. Luke recorded,

> Suddenly, an angel of the Lord appeared among them, and the radi-
> ance of the Lord's glory surrounded them. They were terrified, but
> the angel reassured them. "Don't be afraid!" he said. "I bring you
> good news that will bring great joy to all people. The Savior—yes,
> the Messiah, the Lord—has been born today in Bethlehem,
> the city of David!" (Luke 2:9-11).

Initially, instead of being excited, the shepherds were afraid—terrified, even. Evidently the angel was right there with them and radiated a bright light like they had never seen, and it was scary.

But the good news of Jesus replaced their fear with joy. What was this good news? "The Savior—yes, the Messiah, the Lord—has been born today." The good news was that the Messiah the Jews had been expecting for centuries was born that very night.

When the shepherds checked it out for themselves, they found that what the angel had told them was true, so they returned to their flocks, "glorifying and praising God for all they had heard and seen" (Luke 2:20). They couldn't keep what they had seen to themselves. They told everyone what happened. "And all who heard it wondered at what the shepherds told them" (Luke 2:18, ESV). That word *wondered* means that the people who heard about it marveled—they were blown away.

The reason we celebrate Christmas is that we are *still* blown away by the incredible news that God became a baby that night in Bethlehem. And when we grow in our understanding of what this means, we begin to experience the great joy the angels talked about.

PRAYER

We hear the good news about you, Jesus. Help us to see how good it is so we can experience the joy of your coming.

✦ ✦ ✦

Discussion Starters

- *What do you think it would be like to see an angel?*

- *What made the coming of Jesus such good news for "all people"?*

- *Do you think it is sometimes hard to be filled with joy at the Good News of Jesus? Why is that?*

More from the Bible about—
HOW JOY IS CONNECTED TO JESUS:
Simeon blessed them, and he said to Mary, the baby's mother, "This child is destined to cause many in Israel to fall, but he will be a joy to many others. He has been sent as a sign from God, but many will oppose him." LUKE 2:34

When you obey my commandments, you remain in my love, just as I obey my Father's commandments and remain in his love. I have told you these things so that you will be filled with my joy. Yes, your joy will overflow! JOHN 15:10-11

Are there any wrapped packages under the Christmas tree at your house yet? Won't it be fun to tear off the paper so that what's inside will be revealed for everybody to see?

A long, long time before Jesus was born, the prophet Isaiah wrote, "The glory of the LORD will be revealed, and all people will see it together" (Isaiah 40:5). Like a present is unwrapped, revealing what is inside, Isaiah was saying that the glory of God would be "unwrapped" so that everyone could see what it really looked like.

What is the "glory of the LORD"? The glory of the Lord is the expression of who God is, the demonstration of his character. It is the beauty and brightness of God made visible. This is what happened that night so long ago when the shepherds were guarding their sheep. It seemed like an ordinary night—just like so many nights before out in the fields. But then, "suddenly, an angel of the Lord appeared among them, and the radiance of the Lord's glory surrounded them" (Luke 2:9).

God made his glory visible—in fact, it surrounded the shepherds. It was as if God pulled back the wrapping of the heavens so that God's glory spilled out and around those simple shepherds. What they saw was a glory that has always been there but is usually hidden from human view.

The writer to the Hebrews wrote that Jesus "*radiates* God's own glory and *expresses the very character of God*" (Hebrews 1:3, emphasis added). Glory is to God what brightness is to the sun. We "see" the sun by means of seeing its rays. The round ball of fire in the sky is the sun streaming forth in its radiance. Similarly, we see God the Father by seeing Jesus. Jesus is the radiance of God streaming down on us so we can see God and experience God and know God.

While God's people had seen glimpses of the glory of God before Jesus' birth, they had never seen it so clearly or so brightly. The birth of Christ was the revelation—or the unwrapping—of the glory of the Lord. By faith we too can see this glory. And the day will come when Christ will return and we will see his glory with our eyes.

PRAYER

Give us eyes to see your glory, God,
as we focus on who Jesus is and what he did for us.

✦ ✦ ✦

Discussion Starters

- Luke wrote that the shepherds were terrified when God's glory was revealed. What might have made it so scary?

- Why do you think God's glory is usually hidden from human view?

- Read 2 Corinthians 3:18. Where is the glory of God being revealed, and what does that mean?

More from the Bible about—
GOD'S GLORY DISPLAYED IN JESUS:
God, who said, "Let there be light in the darkness," has made this light shine in our hearts so we could know the glory of God that is seen in the face of Jesus Christ.   2 CORINTHIANS 4:6

Be very glad—for these trials make you partners with Christ in his suffering, so that you will have the wonderful joy of seeing his glory when it is revealed to all the world.   1 PETER 4:13

Remembering How God Has Prepared Our Hearts Year to Year

COMMENTS MADE AND QUESTIONS ASKED
DURING OUR FAMILY'S DEVOTIONS DURING ADVENT

_____

_____

_____

_____

_____

_____

_____

_____

_____

_____

_____

_____

_____

_____

_____

_____

_____

_____

When the angel appeared to the shepherds to tell them about the Savior born in Bethlehem, he brought an army with him. But it wasn't an army of soldiers. Luke wrote, "Suddenly, the angel was joined by a vast host of others—the armies of heaven—praising God and saying, 'Glory to God in highest heaven, and peace on earth to those with whom God is pleased'" (Luke 2:13-14). The angel came with an army of angels.

Usually when we think about an army, we think of war, not peace, right? But that night heaven began to invade earth—not to fight against us or destroy us, but to save us. Isaiah prophesied that Jesus would be the "Prince of Peace," and that the peace he would bring would last forever (Isaiah 9:6-7). Jesus didn't come to destroy his enemies, but to make peace with them. He came to turn his enemies into friends.

We probably have never thought of ourselves as enemies of God. But the Bible says that whether we realize it or not, all of us, at one point, were God's enemies. Left on our own, we are sinners who naturally fight against God. That makes him our enemy. But God has not left us on our own. Even though we have declared war on him deep in our hearts, he has declared peace with us. This friendship is made possible not because Jesus was born, but because Jesus would die. Paul wrote, "Since our friendship with God was restored by the death of his Son while we were still his enemies, we will certainly be saved through the life of his Son" (Romans 5:10).

God does not want to wage war against us even though we've been rebellious toward him. Instead, he has reached out to us, making the first move toward peace. He gives us the grace to overcome our natural resistance toward him so that we can develop a deep friendship with him. He gives us the faith to trust in him, making us one of "those with whom God is pleased."

Thank you, Jesus, for coming to make peace rather than to make war. You have come to announce peace to those with whom God is pleased, and we know that it is only because we are yours that we are pleasing to God. So we come to you and celebrate that we have been joined to you by faith.

✦ ✦ ✦

Discussion Starters

- What is the difference between a friend and an enemy?

- In what way(s) did Jesus bring "peace on earth"?

- What real difference does it make to have our friendship with God restored and to no longer be his enemy?

More from the Bible about—
THE PEACE JESUS BRINGS:
Since we have been made right in God's sight by faith, we have peace with God because of what Jesus Christ our Lord has done for us. Because of our faith, Christ has brought us into this place of undeserved privilege where we now stand, and we confidently and joyfully look forward to sharing God's glory.   ROMANS 5:1-2

God in all his fullness was pleased to live in Christ, and through him God reconciled everything to himself. He made peace with everything in heaven and on earth by means of Christ's blood on the cross. This includes you who were once far away from God. You were his enemies, separated from him by your evil thoughts and actions. Yet now he has reconciled you to himself through the death of Christ in his physical body.   COLOSSIANS 1:19-22

He Became Poor

Who has asked you what you want for Christmas this year? Since we are asked this question from an early age, it is easy for Christmas to become all about *getting* rather than *giving*. Wouldn't a better question to ask each other be, "What are you *giving* for Christmas?" Giving is what Christmas is all about, and we see that when we look at what Jesus did in coming to earth. He did not come to get something from us, but to give us everything that has real and lasting value.

God made the universe. Long before God the Son came to earth, everything was his. The glory and joy of heaven were his. The power and privilege of heaven were his. In heaven he was rich in his relationship with his Father and the Spirit. But to come to earth, he left it all behind. Paul wrote, "You know the generous grace of our Lord Jesus Christ. Though he was rich, yet for your sakes he became poor, so that by his poverty he could make you rich" (2 Corinthians 8:9).

Jesus gave up the riches of heaven to become a poor carpenter on earth. He gave up his close relationship with his Father when he took our sin upon himself on the Cross. In this way, he became poor so that we could become rich. Not wealthy, but rich spiritually. Because he became poor, we can enjoy the richness of a satisfying, saving relationship with God forever.

These riches are available, however, only to those who recognize how poor they are apart from Christ. He does not give his riches to people who think they are already good enough for God and who are satisfied with what they have in this world. Jesus said, "God blesses those who are poor and realize their need for him" (Matthew 5:3).

It is seeing this generosity of Jesus that turns selfish people into joyful givers. We tend toward selfishness because we believe the lie that keeping more for ourselves will make us happy. But Jesus shows us that what will truly make us happy is to become generous givers—like he is.

PRAYER

Jesus, you were rich, but you became poor for us.
You took on our poverty of spirit and you have promised
to share your inheritance with us. So we will not be stingy
with those around us. You have provided us with
everything of true and lasting value.

✦ ✦ ✦

Discussion Starters

- What does it mean to be rich, and what does it mean to be poor?

- What are some of the ways Jesus enjoyed being rich in heaven, and in what ways was he poor while on earth?

- How can seeing the generosity of Jesus help us to be more generous this Christmas season?

More from the Bible about—
THE RICHES GIVEN TO US THROUGH CHRIST:
We are ignored, even though we are well known. We live close to death, but we are still alive. We have been beaten, but we have not been killed. Our hearts ache, but we always have joy. We are poor, but we give spiritual riches to others. We own nothing, and yet we have everything.   2 CORINTHIANS 6:9-10

This same God who takes care of me will supply all your needs from his glorious riches, which have been given to us in Christ Jesus.   PHILIPPIANS 4:19

Thou Didst Leave Thy Throne

1. Thou didst leave Thy throne and Thy king - ly crown, When Thou cam - est to earth for me; But in Beth - le - hem's home was there found no room For Thy ho - ly na - tiv - i - ty. O come to my heart, Lord Je - sus, There is room in my heart for Thee.

2. Heav - en's arch - es rang when the an - gels sang, Pro - claim - ing Thy roy - al de - gree; But of low - ly birth didst Thou come to earth, And in great hu - mil - i - ty. O come to my heart, Lord Je - sus, There is room in my heart for Thee.

3. When the heav'ns shall ring, and her choirs shall sing, At Thy com - ing to vic - to - ry, Let Thy voice call me home, say - ing "Yet there is room, There is room at My side for thee." My heart shall re - joice, Lord Je - sus, When Thou com - est and call - est for me.

Remembering How God Has Prepared Our Hearts Year to Year

COMMENTS MADE AND QUESTIONS ASKED
DURING OUR FAMILY'S DEVOTIONS DURING ADVENT

_____

_____

_____

_____

_____

_____

_____

_____

_____

_____

_____

_____

_____

_____

_____

_____

_____

_____

_____

_____

Seeing and Believing

Think about a time when someone told you something that seemed so incredible you said, "I will have to see it to believe it." It must have been that sense of amazement and curiosity that caused the shepherds to hurry to Bethlehem. Luke wrote:

> When the angels had returned to heaven, the shepherds said to each other, "Let's go to Bethlehem! Let's see this thing that has happened, which the Lord has told us about." They hurried to the village and found Mary and Joseph. And there was the baby, lying in the manger. After seeing him, the shepherds told everyone what had happened and what the angel had said to them about this child. (Luke 2:15-17)

Don't you wish there had been a modern-day news crew on the scene so we could see what the shepherds saw? While we see pretty Christmas cards drawn of this scene with a glow around the baby and his mother, the truth is that the baby Jesus looked like an ordinary infant, and his parents like ordinary people. The shepherds believed what the angels told them about this ordinary-looking baby, and because they believed, the baby became their Savior. Their lives were never the same after seeing and believing in Jesus.

But it must have been difficult for them when they "told everyone what had happened and what the angel had said to them about this child" (Luke 2:17). Apparently "all who heard the shepherds' story were astonished" (Luke 2:18). The story the shepherds told was so amazing and unusual, many must have found it hard to believe. Some people probably said, "That sounds crazy." Some people probably shrugged their shoulders, saying, "That's interesting, but I don't need anybody to save me—especially a baby." But others believed that Jesus was the one God promised to send so long ago, and because they believed, their lives were completely changed.

We all have the same choice to make when we hear the astonishing news that God became a baby and that he is the only Savior. Our reaction to this astonishing news is all-important. Will we shrug our shoulders in disbelief, or will we bend our knees and believe in our hearts?

PRAYER
Jesus, we have never seen you with our physical eyes, but by faith we see you with spiritual eyes, and we believe.

✦ ✦ ✦

Discussion Starters

- *What do you think it looked like, felt like, and smelled like in the place where Jesus was born?*

- *Imagine what kinds of comments the people who listened to the shepherds might have said about their story. How do you imagine the shepherds might have responded?*

- *The shepherds got to see Jesus and therefore believed. But we have not seen Jesus with our eyes, and yet we choose to believe. How is it possible to believe in Jesus without seeing him with our eyes?*

More from the Bible about—
THE CONNECTION OF SEEING AND BELIEVING IN THE BIBLE:
[Jesus] said to Thomas, "Put your finger here, and look at my hands. Put your hand into the wound in my side. Don't be faithless any longer. Believe!" "My Lord and my God!" Thomas exclaimed. Then Jesus told him, "You believe because you have seen me. Blessed are those who believe without seeing me." JOHN 20:27-29

A Birthday Present for Jesus

Most of us have a little list going this time of year—if not on paper, then in our heads. It's that list of what we're hoping someone might give us for Christmas. But isn't it interesting that at Christmas *we* get gifts on someone *else's* birthday? Jesus is the real birthday boy. Have you ever thought about what Jesus might want for his birthday this Christmas?

The Bible tells us that after Jesus was born, "some wise men from eastern lands arrived in Jerusalem, asking, 'Where is the newborn king of the Jews? We saw his star as it rose, and we have come to worship him'" (Matthew 2:1-2).

An unusual star in the sky led these men to Jesus. Matthew wrote that "when they saw the star, they rejoiced *exceedingly with great joy*" (Matthew 2:10, NASB, emphasis added). It's almost as if there aren't enough words to express how much joy they felt over this star that would lead them to Jesus.

When the wise men saw Jesus, they bowed down and worshiped him. And they gave him expensive gifts. Giving is part of worship. If we really admire and love the one we are worshiping, we are glad to give ourselves, and whatever we have of value, to him. If Christ is the true object of our worship, then no one has to force us to worship him or give of ourselves to him. It is what we want to do.

Since it is Jesus' birthday that we celebrate at Christmas, perhaps you should consider what *you* could give to Jesus for his birthday present. Perhaps the gift you could give to Jesus this Christmas is to say to him from your heart, "I'm so happy you brought me to you! You are worthy of my worship, and I want you to be the King of my life. You are more precious to me than anything I own, and I gladly give you the honor you deserve." That is a gift he will enjoy.

We seek after you and bow before you, Jesus.
You are worthy of our worship. We give ourselves and
our worship as our gifts to you.

✦ ✦ ✦

Discussion Starters

- *Instead of thinking only about what you want to get this Christmas, what gifts would you like to give?*

- *What does it mean to "worship" something or someone?*

- *What gift could you give to Jesus this Christmas that would make him happy? And would it make you happy to give it to him?*

More from the Bible about—
GIVING TO JESUS:
Peter said, "We've left our homes to follow you." "Yes," Jesus replied, "and I assure you that everyone who has given up house or wife or brothers or parents or children, for the sake of the Kingdom of God, will be repaid many times over in this life, and will have eternal life in the world to come." LUKE 18:28-30

A poor widow came and dropped in two small coins. Jesus called his disciples to him and said, "I tell you the truth, this poor widow has given more than all the others who are making contributions. For they gave a tiny part of their surplus, but she, poor as she is, has given everything she had to live on." MARK 12:42-44

Born to Die

When a baby is born, people usually celebrate and talk about the long life ahead for that child. But from his birth—even before his birth—a cloud of death loomed over the baby Jesus. This was a baby who was born to die.

The wise men who followed the star to find Jesus seemed to know some things about the Old Testament prophecies about the Messiah. When they came to see Jesus, they actually fulfilled one of those prophecies. Isaiah had written about the Messiah, "Mighty kings will come to see your radiance. . . . [They] will bring gold and frankincense and will come worshiping the LORD" (Isaiah 60:3, 6). Matthew recorded that the wise men "entered the house and saw the child with his mother, Mary, and . . . they opened their treasure chests and gave him gifts of gold, frankincense, and myrrh" (Matthew 2:11).

Gold, frankincense, and myrrh are certainly unusual gifts for a baby! Gold was a gift suited to a king. The wise men must have recognized Jesus as King and so they brought him gold and bowed down to him. Frankincense was a perfume mixed with ground wheat or barley for the grain offering. Frankincense gave off an aroma that was pleasing to God as it burned. This, too, was an appropriate gift for Jesus, who in his life, but especially in his death, would be a pleasing sacrifice to God.

The third gift the wise men brought to Jesus was especially unusual. Myrrh is a sweet-smelling substance that was used to preserve dead bodies and overcome the smell of decay. Why give myrrh to a baby? Perhaps the wise men also understood Isaiah's prophecy that "it was the LORD's good plan to crush him and cause him grief. Yet when his life is made an offering for sin, he will have many descendants" (Isaiah 53:10). The Messiah came as a baby for the very purpose of dying as a sacrifice for sin.

Because Jesus was born to die, we don't have to be afraid of death. Yes, we will all die someday. But if we belong to Jesus, he will one day resurrect our dead bodies and make them new so that we will live with him forever.

PRAYER

Jesus, you were born to die so that we might live!
So even as we prepare to celebrate your birth, we remember
your death. What began in a cradle made of wood culminated
on a cross made of wood. There you defeated sin so that
we can come to God with clean hands.

✦ ✦ ✦

Discussion Starters

- What kinds of gifts do people usually give newborn babies?

- Read Luke 2:34-35. How do Simeon's words to Mary also reveal that Jesus was born to die?

- Why do you think the Gospel writers gave us details that point to Jesus' death from the very beginning of his life?

More from the Bible about—
JESUS' UNDERSTANDING THAT HE WAS BORN TO DIE:
Jesus began to tell his disciples plainly that it was necessary for him to go to Jerusalem, and that he would suffer many terrible things at the hands of the elders, the leading priests, and the teachers of religious law. He would be killed, but on the third day he would be raised from the dead. MATTHEW 16:21

Jesus replied, "Now the time has come for the Son of Man to enter into his glory. I tell you the truth, unless a kernel of wheat is planted in the soil and dies, it remains alone. But its death will produce many new kernels—a plentiful harvest of new lives. Those who love their life in this world will lose it. Those who care nothing for their life in this world will keep it for eternity." JOHN 12:23-25

Hark, the Herald Angels Sing

1. Hark! The her-ald an-gels sing, "Glo-ry to the new-born King; Peace on earth, and mer-cy mild, God and sin-ners rec-on-ciled!" Joy-ful, all ye na-tions rise, Join the tri-umph of the skies; With th'an-gel-ic host pro-claim, "Christ is born in Beth-le-hem!" Hark! the her-ald an-gels sing, "Glo-ry to the new-born King!"

2. Christ, by high-est Heav'n a-dored; Christ the ev-er-last-ing Lord! Late in time, be-hold Him come, Off-spring of a vir-gin's womb. Veiled in flesh the God-head see; Hail th'in-car-nate De-i-ty, Pleased with us in flesh to dwell, Je-sus our Em-man-u-el.

3. Hail the heav'n-ly Prince of Peace! Hail the Sun of Righ-teous-ness! Light and life to all He brings, Ris'n with heal-ing in His wings. Mild He lays His glo-ry by, Born that man no more may die. Born to raise the sons of earth, Born to give them sec-ond birth.

Hark is not a word we use these days. But with this word, the writer of this Christmas carol, Charles Wesley, was simply telling us to listen. He was saying, "Listen to the important news the angels are telling." What were the angels saying? Their message was, "Glory to the newborn King." The angels were announcing the birth of a King.

With the words "peace on earth, and mercy mild," the author was elaborating on this message brought by the angels to the shepherds. He was telling us that this King's heralds were not bringing a message of war, but a message of peace. They were not announcing a message of condemnation and judgment, but a message of mercy. This was not bad news; it was good news—the best news ever!

How would this peace come about? "God and sinners reconciled!" This is what makes Christmas worth celebrating. It is what Jesus came to do. This baby would do what was necessary so that people would not have to be alienated from God because of their sin. Jesus took on himself the punishment for sin so that God would not have to punish us. Instead of experiencing his judgment, we can experience his mercy. Because of what Christ accomplished on the Cross, we can be friends with God instead of his enemies.

In the Scriptures, when someone comes into the presence of God, they stand up—and very often they take off their shoes. So Wesley wrote, "Joyful, all ye nations rise," calling everyone to stand up to honor the coming of Jesus. "Join the triumph of the skies" invites everyone to not just stand but also to respond to this news. Rather than see it as news for somebody else, we are to join in so that Christ and what he accomplished on earth will become personal to us.

The next two stanzas of this song focus on the person of Jesus and the work he accomplished.

"Christ, by highest Heav'n adored" says that the Messiah is worshiped by the greatest created beings. Think of it! This baby in a manger in Bethlehem has been adored by the greatest created beings that exist.

The words "late in time, behold Him come" do not mean that Jesus was late showing up or that somehow he missed his schedule. Instead, after many hundreds of years of his people's waiting, at the right time, the time of God's appointment, the Messiah came into this world. And he came in the most remarkable way—as the "offspring of a virgin's womb."

"Veiled in flesh the Godhead see" means that when we look at Jesus, we are seeing God himself. He took on a body made of skin and bones. Jesus is both completely human and completely God.

The next phrase, "Hail th'incarnate Deity," describes us acknowledging Jesus and recognizing that he is God in the flesh. We don't welcome him merely as a good teacher or as a wise person, but as God.

Jesus is "pleased with us in flesh to dwell." Jesus became a human person not because he was forced to, but because he wanted to.

Then, for the first time in this carol, we sing the name *Jesus*. We've sung about him as King, Christ (Messiah), Lord, Incarnate Deity, and now we sing that Jesus is "our Emmanuel." Jesus is "God with us."

The third stanza, again all about Jesus Christ, reminds us of things the prophets had said about the Messiah long before his coming.

"Hail the heav'nly Prince of Peace!" The prophet Isaiah described the Messiah as the Prince of Peace (Isaiah 9:6).

"Hail the Sun of Righteousness!" The prophet Malachi described the Messiah as "the Sun of Righteousness" who "will rise with healing in his wings" (Malachi 4:2). Jesus is the "Sun of Righteousness," who after centuries of darkness shined a light that radiates healing and wholeness to God's people. "Light and life to all He brings."

When Charles Wesley wrote, "Mild He lays His glory by," he was likely thinking of Philippians 2:7, which says that Jesus "gave up his divine privileges . . . and was born as a human being." Jesus left behind the glory he had in heaven to become an ordinary human with a clear purpose: he was "born that man no more may die." Ever since Adam and Eve sinned, people are born and then they die. But Jesus came to put an end to that. On the Cross he did what was needed to put an end to death, and the day is coming when all those who are connected to Jesus by faith will have bodies that will never die.

Though all people were once physically alive but dead spiritually, Jesus was "born to give them second birth." Jesus has made it possible for spiritually dead people to be born a second time—to be alive spiritually— so that even though our bodies may die, we die with the confidence that Jesus will "raise the sons of earth" from our graves so that we "no more may die."

Remembering How God Has Prepared Our Hearts Year to Year

COMMENTS MADE AND QUESTIONS ASKED
DURING OUR FAMILY'S DEVOTIONS DURING ADVENT

_____

_____

_____

_____

_____

_____

_____

_____

_____

_____

_____

_____

_____

_____

_____

_____

_____

_____

_____

When you're really in trouble, you want someone strong to show up to save you—a real hero. And as people living in this world, we are really in trouble, really in need of someone who can save us from our slavery to sin. God sent someone to save us. The prophet Isaiah wrote about him:

> For a child is born to us, a son is given to us. The government will rest on his shoulders. And he will be called: Wonderful Counselor, Mighty God, Everlasting Father, Prince of Peace. His government and its peace will never end. He will rule with fairness and justice from the throne of his ancestor David for all eternity. The passionate commitment of the LORD of Heaven's Armies will make this happen! (Isaiah 9:6-7)

God sent us a Savior in the form of a baby. The prophet Isaiah assured us, however, that Jesus would be no ordinary baby and that he would grow up to be no ordinary man.

As the Wonderful Counselor, he has the best ideas and strategies; he's the wisest and most perfect teacher. If we listen to him, we'll know what to do.

As the Mighty God, he uses his power on our behalf, helping us overcome sin. We can find protection in him when we're tempted.

As the Everlasting Father, he cares for us lovingly, with affection that has no limits. We can entrust ourselves to him.

As the Prince of Peace, he invites us into his Kingdom of full and perfect happiness, giving us the assurance of safety and security. As we submit to him, we will live lives of blessed closeness to him.

The child born to us became our strong deliverer and our source of security and satisfaction forever. The Son given *to* us gave himself *for* us.

PRAYER

Wonderful Counselor, guide us. Mighty God, rule over us.
Everlasting Father, take care of us. Prince of Peace, give us your peace.

✦ ✦ ✦

Discussion Starters

– How are the heroes in some of your favorite stories like Jesus?

– Why do you think God chose to have the powerful Savior come to earth in the form of a helpless baby?

– Wonderful Counselor, Mighty God, Everlasting Father, Prince of Peace. How is each one of these names a special gift to you personally? Which one do you especially need in your life right now?

More from the Bible about—
HOW JESUS IS OUR TRUE HERO:
Since we are surrounded by such a huge crowd of witnesses to the life of faith, let us strip off every weight that slows us down, especially the sin that so easily trips us up. And let us run with endurance the race God has set before us. We do this by keeping our eyes on Jesus, the champion who initiates and perfects our faith. Because of the joy awaiting him, he endured the cross, disregarding its shame. Now he is seated in the place of honor beside God's throne. HEBREWS 12:1-2

Christmas Eve Scripture Reading

From the Gospel of Matthew, chapter 1:

This is how Jesus the Messiah was born. His mother, Mary, was engaged to be married to Joseph. But before the marriage took place, while she was still a virgin, she became pregnant through the power of the Holy Spirit. Joseph, her fiancé, was a good man and did not want to disgrace her publicly, so he decided to break the engagement quietly.

As he considered this, an angel of the Lord appeared to him in a dream. "Joseph, son of David," the angel said, "do not be afraid to take Mary as your wife. For the child within her was conceived by the Holy Spirit. And she will have a son, and you are to name him Jesus, for he will save his people from their sins."

All of this occurred to fulfill the Lord's message through his prophet:

"Look! The virgin will conceive a child!
She will give birth to a son,
and they will call him Immanuel,
which means 'God is with us.'"

When Joseph woke up, he did as the angel of the Lord commanded and took Mary as his wife. But he did not have sexual relations with her until her son was born. And Joseph named him Jesus. (verses 18–25)

From the Gospel of Luke, chapter 1:

In the sixth month of Elizabeth's pregnancy, God sent the angel Gabriel to Nazareth, a village in Galilee, to a virgin named Mary. She was engaged to be married to a man named Joseph, a descendant of King David. Gabriel appeared to her and said, "Greetings, favored woman! The Lord is with you!"

Confused and disturbed, Mary tried to think what the angel could mean. "Don't be afraid, Mary," the angel told her, "for you have found favor with God! You will conceive and give birth to a son, and you will name him Jesus. He will be very great and will be called the Son of the Most High. The Lord God will give him the throne of his ancestor David. And he will reign over Israel forever; his Kingdom will never end!"

Mary asked the angel, "But how can this happen? I am a virgin."

The angel replied, "The Holy Spirit will come upon you, and the power of the Most High will overshadow you. So the baby to be born will be holy, and he will be called the Son of God. What's more, your relative Elizabeth has become pregnant in her old age! People used to say she was barren, but she has conceived a son and is now in her sixth month. For nothing is impossible with God."

Mary responded, "I am the Lord's servant. May everything you have said about me come true." And then the angel left her. (verses 26–38)

Silent Night

1. Si - lent night, ho - ly night,
2. Si - lent night, ho - ly night,
3. Si - lent night, ho - ly night,

All is calm, all is bright
Shep - herds quake at the sight;
Son of God, love's pure light;

Round yon vir - gin moth - er and Child.
Glo - ries stream from heav - en a - far,
Ra - diant beams from Thy ho - ly face

Ho - ly In - fant, so ten - der and mild,
Heav'n - ly hosts sing Al - le - lu - ia!
With the dawn of re - deem - ing grace,

Sleep in heav - en - ly peace,
Christ the Sav - ior is born,
Je - sus, Lord, at Thy birth,

Sleep in heav - en - ly peace.
Christ the Sav - ior is born!
Je - sus, Lord, at Thy birth.

Remembering How God Has Prepared Our Hearts Year to Year

COMMENTS MADE AND QUESTIONS ASKED
DURING OUR FAMILY'S DEVOTIONS DURING ADVENT

_____

_____

_____

_____

_____

_____

_____

_____

_____

_____

_____

_____

_____

_____

_____

_____

_____

_____

_____

Christmas Day Scripture Reading

From the Gospel of Matthew, chapter 2:

Jesus was born in Bethlehem in Judea, during the reign of King Herod. About that time some wise men from eastern lands arrived in Jerusalem, asking, "Where is the newborn king of the Jews? We saw his star as it rose, and we have come to worship him."

King Herod was deeply disturbed when he heard this, as was everyone in Jerusalem. He called a meeting of the leading priests and teachers of religious law and asked, "Where is the Messiah supposed to be born?"

"In Bethlehem in Judea," they said, "for this is what the prophet wrote:

'And you, O Bethlehem in the land of Judah,
are not least among the ruling cities of Judah,
for a ruler will come from you
who will be the shepherd for my people Israel.' "

Then Herod called for a private meeting with the wise men, and he learned from them the time when the star first appeared. Then he told them, "Go to Bethlehem and search carefully for the child. And when you find him, come back and tell me so that I can go and worship him, too!"

After this interview the wise men went their way. And the star they had seen in the east guided them to Bethlehem. It went ahead of them and stopped over the place where the child was. When they saw the star, they were filled with joy! They entered the house and saw the child with his mother, Mary, and they bowed down and worshiped him. Then they opened their treasure chests and gave him gifts of gold, frankincense, and myrrh.

When it was time to leave, they returned to their own country by another route, for God had warned them in a dream not to return to Herod. (verses 1–12)

From the Gospel of Luke, chapter 2:

At that time the Roman emperor, Augustus, decreed that a census should be taken throughout the Roman Empire. (This was the first census taken when Quirinius was governor of Syria.) All returned to their own ancestral towns to register for this census. And because Joseph was a descendant of King David, he had to go to Bethlehem in Judea, David's ancient home. He traveled there from the village of Nazareth in Galilee. He took with him Mary, his fiancée, who was now obviously pregnant.

And while they were there, the time came for her baby to be born. She gave birth to her first child, a son. She wrapped him snugly in strips of cloth and laid him in a manger, because there was no lodging available for them.

That night there were shepherds staying in the fields nearby, guarding their flocks of sheep. Suddenly, an angel of the Lord appeared among them, and the radiance of the Lord's glory surrounded them. They were terrified, but the angel reassured them. "Don't be afraid!" he said. "I bring you good news that will bring great joy to all people. The Savior—yes, the Messiah, the Lord—has been born today in Bethlehem, the city of David! And you will recognize him by this sign: You will find a baby wrapped snugly in strips of cloth, lying in a manger."

Suddenly, the angel was joined by a vast host of others— the armies of heaven—praising God and saying,

"Glory to God in highest heaven,
and peace on earth to those with whom God is pleased."

When the angels had returned to heaven, the shepherds said to each other, "Let's go to Bethlehem! Let's see this thing that has happened, which the Lord has told us about."

They hurried to the village and found Mary and Joseph. And there was the baby, lying in the manger. After seeing him, the shepherds told everyone what had happened and what the angel had said to them about this child. All who heard the shepherds' story were astonished, but Mary kept all these things in her heart and thought about them often. The shepherds went back to their flocks, glorifying and praising God for all they had heard and seen. It was just as the angel had told them. (verses 1–20)

O Come, All Ye Faithful

1. O come, all ye faith - ful, joy - ful and tri - um - phant, O come ye, O come___ ye, to Beth - le - hem. Come and be - hold Him, born the King of an - gels; O come, let us a - dore Him, O come, let us a - dore Him, O come, let us a - dore Him,___ Christ___ the Lord.

2. Yea, Lord, we greet Thee, born this hap - py morn - ing;___ Je - sus, to Thee___ be glo - ry giv'n; Word of the Fa - ther, now in flesh ap - pear - ing. O

What's the best gift you received this Christmas? You can hardly wait to play with it, put it on, or figure it out! When we receive a gift that pleases us, we want to enjoy it and share it with others.

God is the most generous Giver in the universe, and he has given us the most valuable gift in the universe—Jesus himself. John wrote, "From his abundance we have all received one gracious blessing after another" (John 1:16). God knows just what to give us, just what we need most, and that is Jesus. It is the greatness of this gift that prompts us to give each other gifts at Christmas.

But some people don't realize how beautiful and valuable the gift of Jesus is, and so they never truly receive him.

Sometimes we are given a gift that we think is not really useful to us, and therefore we never take it out of the box. We stash it away in a closet or on a shelf somewhere in case we need it someday. Sadly, that's what some people do in regard to Jesus. They want to keep him handy for when something comes along that they can't handle on their own, but for now they have no interest in making him part of their day-to-day lives, and so they put him on the shelf. They simply don't believe he is as good as the Bible says he is, and so they have no real or lasting joy in having received this great gift.

John wrote, "To all who received him, to those who believed in his name, he gave the right to become children of God" (John 1:12, NIV). God has given us the gift of Jesus, but it is up to each of us to receive that gift, unwrap that gift, make that gift a part of our daily lives. To receive Christ is to recognize that he is the most beautiful, most desirable treasure in the universe and open up our lives to him, saying, "I must have him!"

PRAYER

*Jesus, we receive you! We welcome you into our home
and into our hearts this Christmas. Show us what it means
to unwrap this incredible gift we've been given and put
you at the very center of our day-to-day lives.*

✦ ✦ ✦

Discussion Starters

– What are some of your favorite gifts that you've received? How do
  these gifts show that the people who gave them knew what you
  wanted or needed?

– How have you enjoyed the generosity of God over this past year?

– How does Romans 8:32 (below) encourage you as you think about
  needs you have in the coming year?

More from the Bible about—
THE GOOD GIFTS GOD GIVES:
I tell you, keep on asking, and you will receive what you ask for.
Keep on seeking, and you will find. Keep on knocking, and the door
will be opened to you. For everyone who asks, receives. Everyone
who seeks, finds. And to everyone who knocks, the door will be
opened. You fathers—if your children ask for a fish, do you give
them a snake instead? Or if they ask for an egg, do you give them
a scorpion? Of course not! So if you sinful people know how to
give good gifts to your children, how much more will your heavenly
Father give the Holy Spirit to those who ask him.   LUKE 11:9-13

Since [God] did not spare even his own Son but gave him up for us
all, won't he also give us everything else?   ROMANS 8:32

Remembering How God Has
Prepared Our Hearts Year to Year

COMMENTS MADE AND QUESTIONS ASKED
DURING OUR FAMILY'S DEVOTIONS DURING ADVENT

_____

_____

_____

_____

_____

_____

_____

_____

_____

_____

_____

_____

_____

_____

_____

_____

_____

_____

Eagerly Waiting

It's hard to wait—especially when you really want something and you've been disappointed over and over while waiting for it. Sometimes disappointment makes you want to give up and stop wanting it so much. That's what many people did before Jesus came—they gave up waiting for and wanting a messiah to come and deliver them. They got tired of the wait, so they stopped looking and longing. They stopped expecting that God would fulfill his promise.

But not everybody got tired of waiting. Luke 2 tells about two people— Simeon and Anna—who were still eagerly waiting and watching for the promised Messiah.

At that time there was a man in Jerusalem named Simeon. He was righteous and devout and was eagerly waiting for the Messiah to come and rescue Israel. The Holy Spirit was upon him and had revealed to him that he would not die until he had seen the Lord's Messiah. That day the Spirit led him to the Temple. So when Mary and Joseph came to present the baby Jesus to the Lord as the law required, Simeon was there. He took the child in his arms and praised God, saying,

"Sovereign Lord, now let your servant die in peace,
  as you have promised.
I have seen your salvation,
  which you have prepared for all people.
He is a light to reveal God to the nations,
  and he is the glory of your people Israel!"

Jesus' parents were amazed at what was being said about him. Then Simeon blessed them, and he said to Mary, the baby's mother, "This child is destined to cause many in Israel to fall, but he will be a joy to many others. He has been sent as a sign from God, but many will oppose him. As a result, the deepest thoughts of many hearts will be revealed. And a sword will pierce your very soul."

Anna, a prophet, was also there in the Temple. She was the daughter of Phanuel from the tribe of Asher, and she was very old. Her husband died when they had been married only seven years. Then she lived as a widow to the age of eighty-four. She never left the Temple but stayed there day and night, worshiping God with fasting and prayer. She came along just as Simeon was talking with Mary and Joseph, and she began praising God. She talked about the child to everyone who had been waiting expectantly for God to rescue Jerusalem. (Luke 2:25-38)

When Simeon saw the baby Jesus, he knew the wait was over. And when Anna heard what Simeon said, she shared it with everyone else she knew who was waiting expectantly.

Once again we are in a period of waiting—waiting for Jesus to come a second time. And we can expect that, like the first time, Jesus will be revealed to those who are waiting eagerly to see him. It might seem like it will never happen, and the world thinks it's ridiculous to be looking for Jesus' arrival. But we continue waiting and watching.

PRAYER

We eagerly wait for you, Jesus, to come again. Our hearts are set on you, longing for your soon return. Come quickly, Lord Jesus!

+ + +

Discussion Starters

– When have you found it especially hard to wait?

– What did Simeon celebrate about Jesus? What did he prophesy about Jesus?

– What are things that drain us of our longing for Jesus' return? How can we nurture an eager longing for his return?

More from the Bible about—
WAITING FOR JESUS TO RETURN:
The grace of God that brings salvation has appeared to all men. It teaches us to say "No" to ungodliness and worldly passions, and to live self-controlled, upright and godly lives in this present age, while we wait for the blessed hope—the glorious appearing of our great God and Savior, Jesus Christ, who gave himself for us to redeem us from all wickedness and to purify for himself a people that are his very own, eager to do what is good. TITUS 2:11-14, NIV

Now the prize awaits me—the crown of righteousness, which the Lord, the righteous Judge, will give me on the day of his return. And the prize is not just for me but for all who eagerly look forward to his appearing. 2 TIMOTHY 4:8

Joy to the World

1. Joy to the world, the Lord is come! Let earth receive her King;_____ Let ev - 'ry_____ heart_____ pre - pare_____ Him_____ room,_____ And Heav'n and na - ture_____ sing, And_____ Heav'n and na - ture_____ sing, And_____ Heav'n,_____ and Heav'n,_____ and na - ture sing.

2. No more let sins and sor - rows grow, Nor thorns in - fest the ground;_____ He comes to_____ make_____ His bless - ings_____ flow_____ Far as the curse is_____ found, Far_____ as the curse is_____ found, Far_____ as,_____ far as,_____ the curse is found.

3. He rules the world with truth and grace, And makes the na - tions prove_____ The glo - ries_____ of_____ His right - eous - ness,_____ And won - ders of His_____ love, And_____ won - ders of His_____ love, And_____ won - ders,_____ won - ders, of His love.

In the 1700s, when Isaac Watts lived, most people in their worship service sang psalms from the Bible set to music. Watts didn't think that the psalms that had been arranged for singing were very good, so he set about the task of trying to do a better job. The song we sing as "Joy to the World" is Isaac Watts's rendering of Psalm 98.

Psalm 98 is about the coming of the Lord. It is not immediately clear as to whether it's about the first coming of Christ or about his second coming. But in light of what we know concerning what Jesus did in his first coming and what he said would happen at his second coming, we know that this section of Psalm 98, and therefore the entire song "Joy to the World," is about the second coming of Jesus.

We know this is not about his first coming because when Jesus came the first time, he was not received by all, creation didn't sing out for him, and sin and sorrow and all the effects of the curse were still the reality that people lived in—and that we still, in fact, live in. All the nations of the world did not yet submit to his rule.

But when Christ comes again, all these things will be different. Every knee will bow to him; there will be no more resistance to him. It won't be just people who will celebrate his coming; the earth itself will celebrate. The curse will finally be gone so that all of creation will be set free from decay to worship Christ. People from every tribe and nation will gladly crown him as King. This is why there is so much joy in "Joy to the World"! It is not so much about the joy of Christ's coming the *first* time, but it anticipates the joy when Christ will come the *second* time—when the Kingdom he established at his first coming will be the reality we will live in forever.

When we understand what we're saying when we sing this song, we realize that this song celebrates the essence of our Christian hope as believers. Our hope is not simply looking back to treasure Christ's birth or seeing what Christ accomplished on the Cross. It is not only in our experience here and now of Christ changing us as we put our faith in him. Our greatest joy is centered on our future hope of the day when Christ will return in glory to this earth. On that day, all who are dead in Christ will be resurrected. This is what we read in Revelation 21:1-5 about the day that "Joy to the World" celebrates:

Then I saw a new heaven and a new earth, for the old heaven and the old earth had disappeared. And the sea was also gone. And I saw the holy city, the new Jerusalem, coming down from God out of heaven like a bride beautifully dressed for her husband.

I heard a loud shout from the throne, saying, "Look, God's home is now among his people! He will live with them, and they will be his people. God himself will be with them. He will wipe every tear from their eyes, and there will be no more death or sorrow or crying or pain. All these things are gone forever."

And the one sitting on the throne said, "Look, I am making everything new!"

That day, described in Psalm 98 and sung about in "Joy to the World," will be a great day! Because God fulfilled his promises to send Jesus the first time, we can sing "Joy to the World" confidently and expectantly, sure that he will come again.

Remembering How God Has Prepared Our Hearts Year to Year

COMMENTS MADE AND QUESTIONS ASKED
DURING OUR FAMILY'S DEVOTIONS DURING ADVENT

_____

_____

_____

_____

_____

_____

_____

_____

_____

_____

_____

_____

_____

_____

_____

_____

_____

_____

_____

Pretty soon it will be time to take down the Christmas lights and put away the decorations. January will be here, and this Christmas will be a memory. If we're not careful, ordinary life can cause us to lose our sense of wonder over Jesus' coming.

That might have happened on the first Christmas, too. Though it seems like everyone would have kept their eyes on a baby whose birth had been announced by a sky full of angels, evidently people lost interest. The shepherds had to go back to taking care of their sheep. The wise men went back to their own country. It seems most people set aside their hopes that this baby could make a difference in the world.

"All who heard the shepherds' story were astonished, but Mary kept all these things in her heart and thought about them often" (Luke 2:18-19). Other translations say that Mary "pondered" all the things she heard and experienced. Though most people who witnessed what happened in Bethlehem may have put it in the back of their minds or out of their minds, Mary continued to really think it over. It was as if she said to herself, "I won't forget hearing the angel. I will remember what it was like to have the Holy Spirit come over me; I will keep the memory close of seeing Jesus worshiped by the wise men."

Though Mary certainly knew this was a child God had given her, and the song she sang celebrated that this baby would be the fulfillment of God's promises to Abraham, evidently she didn't understand everything about Jesus and what he came to do—but she wanted to. So Mary began a process of "connecting the dots" in her own mind, adding up the prophecies about the Messiah from the Old Testament prophets that her son, Jesus, fulfilled at his birth. She must have marveled at this child of hers who never gave in to temptation and seemed to understand the purpose for his life at such a young age. She must have wondered how and when her son would begin to turn the world upside down and how it would impact her entire family.

While others lost interest, Mary thought through everything about who Jesus was, why he came, and what he would accomplish. She thought through what the angel had said to her and to Joseph about Jesus, the song God had given to her, the visits of the shepherds and the wise men. Mary is a good example for us—especially those of us who have heard the Christmas story so many times that we are hardly startled by its startling aspects. We have to think it through, meditating on what it tells us about Jesus, whom God sent to save us.

PRAYER

In the quiet of these days, Lord, we choose to ponder all that
we have read about your coming. Give us eyes to see the wonder
of it and hearts that overflow with the joy of it.

✦ ✦ ✦

Discussion Starters

- *What has been your favorite part of celebrating Christmas this year?*

- *What thoughts do you imagine went through Mary's mind as she tried to make sense of all she'd experienced and witnessed?*

- *What are some ways you can ponder Jesus when you find he is not in your thoughts throughout the day?*

More from the Bible about—
PONDERING CHRIST:

Don't copy the behavior and customs of this world, but let God transform you into a new person by changing the way you think. Then you will learn to know God's will for you, which is good and pleasing and perfect.   ROMANS 12:2

Fix your thoughts on what is true, and honorable, and right, and pure, and lovely, and admirable. Think about things that are excellent and worthy of praise.   PHILIPPIANS 4:8

Since you have been raised to new life with Christ, set your sights on the realities of heaven, where Christ sits in the place of honor at God's right hand. Think about the things of heaven, not the things of earth. For you died to this life, and your real life is hidden with Christ in God.   COLOSSIANS 3:1-3

Think clearly and exercise self-control. Look forward to the gracious salvation that will come to you when Jesus Christ is revealed to the world.   1 PETER 1:13

The Word Became Human

It can be fun to dress up as something we are not. When we put on costumes, it is usually for a brief time, and then we take off the costume and go back to being who we really are. Just because we dress up like a character in a movie or a person from history doesn't mean we actually *become* that character or person.

We might assume that Jesus put on a "costume" of skin to be a human for the thirty-three years he spent on this earth, and then he went back to his "usual" self when he returned to heaven. But Jesus went much further than that. John wrote, "The Word *became* human" (John 1:14, emphasis added). Jesus *became* flesh—forever. He didn't just appear to be human; he *became* human—not just for his brief life on earth, but for all eternity. Even now, Jesus is in heaven at the right hand of God in his post-resurrection, glorified, human body.

Jesus was willing to be human in all its messiness. The Son of God had to let Mary change his diaper. He went through puberty. He was susceptible to disease and had surging hormones. Jesus got hungry and sleepy, his muscles ached after a hard day working in the carpenter's shop, his nose got sunburned, and his lips got chapped.

Jesus became absolutely human, not just in body, but in mind. Jesus went to school as a child. And he didn't sit in the front row with all the answers automatically programmed into him. The Bible says that Jesus learned just like we do: "Jesus grew in wisdom and in stature" (Luke 2:52).

Jesus was also fully human in his emotions. He felt the range of human emotions that we feel. When Lazarus died, Jesus "was deeply moved in spirit and troubled" (John 11:33, NIV). He experienced joy (John 15:11), anger (Mark 3:5), and even surprise (Mark 6:6; Luke 7:9).

While we had no choice about being made of flesh and blood, Jesus chose to be human. While still being completely divine and completely holy, he also willingly took hold of the messiness of being a person. He entered into our reality, walking, breathing, and living in our world. The only thing he did not do is sin. But the most important experience he went through as a human was physical death. This was his ultimate purpose in becoming flesh—so he could die in our place.

PRAYER
Because you became human, Jesus, you understand our struggles. And because, as a human, you died and rose again, we can be confident that we will too!

✦ ✦ ✦

Discussion Starters

- Think about Jesus as a baby and as a young child and teenager. What human things must he have experienced?

- As you consider some of the things that are hard about being human, how does it help to know that Jesus understands because he is human too?

- Jesus not only lived as a human but also died and was resurrected as a human. How does that give us hope?

More from the Bible about—
THE HUMANNESS OF JESUS:
In Christ lives all the fullness of God in a human body. COLOSSIANS 2:9

Because God's children are human beings—made of flesh and blood—the Son also became flesh and blood. For only as a human being could he die, and only by dying could he break the power of the devil, who had the power of death. HEBREWS 2:14

His Two Comings

The Old Testament prophets who wrote about the Messiah's coming saw his coming kind of like we see a range of mountains from far away. They wrote about things that would happen and things the Messiah would do when he came. But from so far away, they couldn't understand that Christ would accomplish some of those things the first time he came and others when he comes again, at a time even further in the future. The prophets couldn't see the immense distances of time that separate one event from another. While being a prophet meant that you had a message from God, it didn't mean you always understood the meaning or the timing of the events predicted.

For example, the prophet Isaiah described the Messiah coming as a child who would be born (Isaiah 9:6), as a servant who would suffer (Isaiah 53), and as a lamb who would be led to the slaughter (Isaiah 53:7). These prophecies were clearly fulfilled by Jesus when he came the first time. But Isaiah also wrote that when the Messiah comes, "the wolf and the lamb will live together" (Isaiah 11:6) and that "he will rule with a powerful arm" (Isaiah 40:10). Isaiah prophesied about a day when "no longer will you need the sun to shine by day, nor the moon to give its light by night, for the LORD your God will be your everlasting light, and your God will be your glory" (Isaiah 60:19). Obviously these prophecies were not fulfilled when Christ came the first time. These are the things we look forward to when he will come the second time.

Many of the Old Testament prophecies about the Messiah are still awaiting fulfillment. So just as the people of Israel longed for the Messiah to come, we long for him to come again. Added to the Old Testament prophecies are all the things Jesus told us about his return—he said the whole world will see his coming on the clouds of heaven with great glory at a time when we least expect it. So Jesus said we must be ready all the time for his return. We don't know *when* it will be, but we know it will be.

PRAYER

Jesus, as we look at all the prophecies you fulfilled in your first coming, it gives us confidence that all the remaining promises about your coming will be fulfilled when you come again. We are longing and looking for that day!

✦ ✦ ✦

Discussion Starters

– *Look up the following prophecies and discuss whether you think they refer to Jesus' first coming, his second coming, or both: Genesis 3:15; Isaiah 9:1-7; Isaiah 52:13–53:12; Jeremiah 23:5-6; Daniel 7:13-14; Zechariah 9:9.*

More from the Bible about—
THE COMING OF JESUS:
The LORD has sent this message to every land: "Tell the people of Israel, 'Look, your Savior is coming. See, he brings his reward with him as he comes.'" ISAIAH 62:11

Just as everyone dies because we all belong to Adam, everyone who belongs to Christ will be given new life. But there is an order to this resurrection: Christ was raised as the first of the harvest; then all who belong to Christ will be raised when he comes back. 1 CORINTHIANS 15:22-23

When he comes on that day, he will receive glory from his holy people—praise from all who believe. 2 THESSALONIANS 1:10

Remembering How God Has Prepared Our Hearts Year to Year

COMMENTS MADE AND QUESTIONS ASKED
DURING OUR FAMILY'S DEVOTIONS DURING ADVENT

_____

_____

_____

_____

_____

_____

_____

_____

_____

_____

_____

_____

_____

_____

_____

_____

_____

_____

_____

_____

As the year comes to a close and we prepare to begin a new year, we know that our family will get busy doing lots of things—many good things. The new beginning that comes with a new year allows us to step back and consider if all the things that we are busy with help us move forward toward what is most important. We want to ask, Are the things we're doing helping us or hindering us from making progress in the one thing that is most important—the one thing that will matter for eternity?

Paul was determined to make sure that everything he was doing helped him in accomplishing the *one thing* that was most important. "I press on to possess that perfection for which Christ Jesus first possessed me," he said. "I focus on this one thing: Forgetting the past and looking forward to what lies ahead, I press on to reach the end of the race and receive the heavenly prize for which God, through Christ Jesus, is calling us" (Philippians 3:12-14). As Paul looked toward the future, he was determined to "press on." He wanted to continue to make progress in the life of faith—to love and trust God more tomorrow than he did yesterday. He wanted to live his life now in light of eternity. He didn't want to become distracted by anything that would steal his attention from what will matter for eternity.

What would it look like to "press on" toward knowing and enjoying Christ as you and your family enter another year? The kind of straining forward Paul wrote about means implementing the self-discipline and self-denial of a serious athlete. It means making plans and setting goals for ourselves in the areas of worship, studying God's Word, developing our prayer lives, and sharing Christ, so that by next year at this time we will be closer to Jesus.

Today is a good day to look back, look forward, and look inward. We want to see ourselves and our lives as Christ sees us and be willing to face hard truths about ourselves. But more important than looking inward is looking upward to Christ. Looking to Christ gives us a goal to pursue, a person to enjoy, a passion to feed. Looking to Christ orients the direction of the coming year—and of our entire lives.

PRAYER

As we look into the coming year, we're pressing on, Lord Jesus. We have fixed our gaze on you and we long for you to become the one thing in our lives that everything else revolves around, the one thing everything else flows from.

✦ ✦ ✦

Discussion Starters

- Think back over the past year together as a family. What individual and family accomplishments are you pleased with? What experiences were especially fun or meaningful?

- How would you put into your own words what the "one thing" was that both Paul and David (Philippians 3:13; Psalm 27:4) devoted their lives to?

- Look ahead into the coming year. What habits do you want to break? What skills would you like to master? What would you like to experience? How can your home become more oriented toward Christ in the coming year?

More from the Bible about—
SINCERELY SEEKING CHRIST INTO ETERNITY:
Let us run with endurance the race God has set before us. We do this by keeping our eyes on Jesus, the champion who initiates and perfects our faith.   HEBREWS 12:1-2

We should live in this evil world with wisdom, righteousness, and devotion to God, while we look forward with hope to that wonderful day when the glory of our great God and Savior, Jesus Christ, will be revealed.   TITUS 2:12-13

About the Author

Nancy Guthrie has a passion for sharing God's Word through her growing national and international Bible teaching ministry. She is the author of *Holding On to Hope, The One Year Book of Hope, Hoping for Something Better, One Year of Dinner Table Devotions and Discussion Starters, Hearing Jesus Speak into Your Sorrow,* and *When Your Family's Lost a Loved One* (cowritten with her husband, David). Nancy lives with her husband and their son, Matt, in Nashville, Tennessee. Visit her Web site at nancyguthrie.com.

Has your family enjoyed talking together about truths from God's Word each day during December? Why not keep it up all year through? *One Year of Dinner Table Devotions and Discussion Starters* by Nancy Guthrie serves up daily truths from God's Word to chew on and apply to real life at a level that kids from elementary age through high school will understand and relate to. Transform family devotions from dry lectures into dynamic conversations as you draw closer to each other—and closer to God himself.

Books by Nancy Guthrie

Holding On to Hope
978-1-4143-1296-5

Hearing Jesus Speak
into Your Sorrow
978-1-4143-2548-4

Hoping for Something Better
978-1-4143-1307-8

When Your Family's
Lost a Loved One
978-1-58997-480-7

The One Year Book of Hope
978-1-4143-0133-4

One Year of Dinner Table
Devotions and Discussion
Starters
978-1-4143-1895-0

Let Every Heart Prepare
Him Room
978-1-4143-6441-4

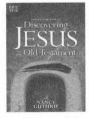

The One Year Book of
Discovering Jesus in the
Old Testament
978-1-4143-3590-2